Bring the Girl Home

Bring the Girl Home

Rebecca Wilson

Copyright © 2024 for title is held by Rebecca Wilson.

All rights reserved. No part of this publication may be reproduced, distributed or transmitted in any form or by any means, including photocopying, recording or other electronic or mechanical methods, without the prior written permission of the publisher, except in the case of brief quotations embodied in critical reviews and certain other noncommercial uses permitted by the copyright law.

For permission requests, write to the publisher at the address below.

E.P. House
www.ephouse.co

This is a work of nonfiction. Nonetheless, some names, identifying details and personal characteristics of the individuals involved have been changed. In addition, certain people who appear in these pages are composites of a number of individuals and their experiences.

The views and ideas expressed in this book are those of the author and do not reflect those of E.P. House.

Library of Congress Cataloging-in-Publication Data is available.

First paperback edition - June 2024
Paperback ISBN: 979-8-8693-3269-1
Digital ISBN: 979-8-8693-3270-7

PRINTED IN THE UNITED STATES OF AMERICA ON ACID-FREE PAPER

Cover Design by Taylor Lisney

*For my daughter, Angelina.
May you know the whole truth one day.
Until we meet again.*

··· Contents

Introduction	*pg. ix*
Chapter One	pg. 15
Chapter Two	pg. 25
Chapter Three	pg. 39
Chapter Four	pg. 55
Chapter Five	pg. 77
Chapter Six	pg. 87
Chapter Seven	pg. 101
Chapter Eight	pg. 117
Chapter Nine	pg. 135
Chapter Ten	pg. 145
Chapter Eleven	pg. 155
Chapter Twelve	pg. 163
Chapter Thirteen	pg. 169
Chapter Fourteen	pg. 201
Chapter Fifteen	pg. 209
Chapter Sixteen	pg. 215
Chapter Seventeen	pg. 225
Chapter Eighteen	pg. 241
About the Author	*pg. 249*

···· Introduction

As a registered nurse, I ask myself daily, how did I ever get to this point in my life? Maybe I do not look like a domestic abuse survivor, but I am. I have survived extreme spousal abuse that consisted of physical, emotional, social, economic, and sexual abuse.

But I was so naïve that I didn't realize any of it.

As a nurse, I have excellent communication skills. I am great at speaking and listening to others, problem solving, and effectively talking and communicating with patients and families. I can advocate for my patients with their needs and concerns. *But why couldn't I do the same for myself?* I was a trauma nurse for years, helping patients to recover from serious accidents and manage their stress from tough situations, helping them to recover both physically and mentally. Work was the only time I could be myself because I was out of his sight. The hospital became my safe haven.

In addition to my other strengths, I also have immense empathy for the pain and suffering of the patients I have cared for. Because I am a great problem solver, I respond quickly to emergencies or other situations that arise. I have always respected others, including the hospital staff and my patients. *So, why would someone with so much knowledge get herself into a tough situation the likes of which I could not escape?* I was constantly torn between trying to create my dream of a loving family and the reality of my situation.

The word "good" means a lack of self-centeredness. A person that is "good" can empathize with others and feel compassion for them. "Good" people put others' needs before their own. They are selfless. I see myself as a "good" person. I have always put others before myself; I am caring and empathetic.

On the opposite end, "evil" means immoral, wicked, and having the will to destroy. So, I often wonder, *what does it mean to be evil? Can a human being truly be evil? Are we born evil, or do we learn to be evil? Are evil people born with a brain disorder? Are we taught our moral beliefs by our parents or by society?*

I wonder because an evil man named Anthony tried to destroy me by stealing time that I will never get back. He stole years when I should have been in college having the time of my life. He stole my moment of turning twenty-one, when I should have celebrated with friends, if I'd had any left. He stole years from early adulthood where I should have been traveling and having fun. Turning thirty should have been an exciting time, but I celebrated alone. I missed countless holidays with my family. I missed the celebration of the birth of my niece. I missed vacations and time with my extended family.

But far worse than all of that—even worse than the beatings and time spent alone—was when he stole my time with my only daughter, the day he kidnapped her and fled the country.

I spent too much time alone, trapped. I lived in a cage built by Anthony, where he was in complete control. He told me when to wake up, go to sleep, eat, work, and clean. It was like living in a prison with invisible shackles. I wore a fake smile every day that broke my heart. And I wore a heavy weight on my soul that slowly lifted once I finally freed myself.

Abuse can affect anyone. It happens to the wealthy and the less fortunate, the highly educated and less educated. Abuse happens in every race, color, and culture. What remains consistent are the warning signs, but most of us are so young and naïve that we do not see the bright red flags frantically waving before us.

I, too, was young and naïve. Abuse was not something I had been exposed to before. It wasn't until I began nursing school that I studied the four stages in the cycle of abuse. At the time, I shook it off and thought *no, this is not me*.

The cycle begins with the "tension building phase" where verbal abuse usually starts. And yes, during this phase I tried to please Anthony. Soon after, the tension built up so high that he flipped out and beat me to a pulp; known as an acute battering episode, which is the "incident of violence phase." Next, is the "reconciliation phase" before the "calm phase," but my abuser never showed sympathy for his actions or had remorse. Even though he would appear to be more loving after the beatings, I realize now that it was all an act. After this phase, leaving was never a choice. I thought that if I loved him enough, he wouldn't hurt me. But this was just an act that played out in my head, it was not reality.

He constantly told me that my family didn't love me or know me the way he did. When times are good—especially in the reconciliation phase—the victim feels a sense of relief and is grateful to the abuser. During those times, I felt safe and believed that it would not happen again. What I did have to get through this tough time of my life was my family and friends, and my job. I do not think I would have escaped from his shackles if I was not a nurse. My coworkers are the people who helped me get out of this nightmare. If it were not for them, I believe that I would still be locked up and living alone. I still sometimes live in the embarrassment and shame of my story, and feeling this way is not something I am alone in. Many survivors struggle with this.

Domestic violence is violent or aggressive behavior within the home, typically involving the violent abuse of a spouse or partner. During my profession as a nurse I took care of many women who I could tell were in abusive relationships, when I was in one myself. As nurses, we ask these patients if they felt safe at home. I truly felt badly for the injuries some had gone through, such as broken bones to having acid thrown in their eyes. It was devastating to see the police take pictures of their bruised bodies, cuts, and broken bones. They would be shaking and crying, asking me why this had happened to them.

I knew my husband beat me, but he only cracked my ribs *slightly*. He only ripped *small* chunks of hair out. He only broke the *septum* of my nose. He *only* knocked the wind out of me, gave me regular concussions, and bloody noses and bruises. At the time, my injuries were not *that* serious. I knew that *that*—what happened to these other women—would never be me. He would *never* go that far.

A sociopath is a person with a personality disorder manifesting itself in extreme antisocial attitudes and behavior and a lack of conscience. Some traits of a sociopath are superficial charm, good intelligence, absence of delusions, signs of irrational thinking, unreliability, untruthfulness and insincerity, lack of remorse and shame, poor judgment, and failure to learn by experience, specific loss of insight, unresponsiveness in general interpersonal relations, sex life impersonal, trivial, and poorly integrated and failure to follow any life plan. Sociopaths will lie and manipulate you with a lack of emotion to follow. This type of person is cold and manipulative and does not care about anyone around them unless it is benefiting them. I believed this information was just in my nursing textbooks. I thought to myself that this type of person is not walking around out there on the street, and that I would never come across them in my lifetime.

People like this, I felt, were either in mental institutions or in prison.

A narcissist has an excessive or erotic interest in themselves and their physical appearance. A narcissistic person will have a grandiose sense of self-importance, is preoccupied with fantasies of unlimited success, power, brilliance, beauty, or ideal love. They will believe that they are "special" and unique and can only be understood by, or should associate with, other special or high-status people. They require excessive admiration. They have a sense of entitlement and are interpersonally exploitative. They lack empathy and often believe that others are envious of him or her. They will show arrogance and rude and abusive behaviors or attitudes.

The most dangerous type of person—in my judgment—is a narcissistic sociopath. They are driven to have destructive power and control over people. They see and love others admiring them as their tools of power to manipulate and take over others. They have not an ounce of guilt or apologies under any wrong or mean actions they have caused. They feel like nothing can stop them and they are invincible. These people feel like they will run the whole show. And this person thought he could run my entire life.

Because, in my medical opinion, Anthony is a narcissistic sociopath.

These words "evil," "sociopath," and "narcissist" never crossed my mind during my time spent with Anthony. The term "narcissistic sociopath" didn't make the perfect sense that it does for me today. For fourteen years of my life, those words consumed me.

"How are you so strong?" people ask.

"How are you able to keep going?"

"If I were you ..."

My answer to these questions is, "because I do not have a choice." I *must* keep fighting. For me, my purpose in life is to be a good mother, wife, and to help others heal. Knowing my purpose in life after living in the control of someone else takes life to another level of understanding our existence. All of this happened to me for a reason. The reason is to help others and to make them understand that there is more to life and happiness. We can never give up, especially when we have children who are looking up to us. Someday happiness will come back to us. Someday we will be able to love and trust again. It may take time, but it will happen.

··· Chapter One

My childhood was nothing but ordinary. I was born in chocolate town, Hershey, Pennsylvania, at the same hospital I still work at. My childhood was filled with the love of a middle-class family, I grew up with both my parents and my younger brother Andrew and my older sister Katie. My grandparents lived close by; they always took us places and spoiled us. My childhood was absent of any type of trauma or horrific experiences. I was not a child with a poor upbringing, or of living in neglect or poverty.

My parents never fought and visibly loved each other. We ate dinner every night as a family, sitting around the dining table. I grew up in a very sheltered world and had no idea that evil existed. We celebrated holidays and birthdays. Eventually, we moved out of Hershey and into a small town out in the country where not much happened. I played outside in the woods building forts and exploring with my friend Jess, who I have known since preschool. Our homes were within walking distance. Her mom was the best babysitter to my brother and I growing up. We rode the school bus every morning, and after school, sports and afterschool activities followed.

I attended this school and had the same friends up until high school graduation. Every Friday night we all went to the high school football games to cheer on our school. A group of my friends that I grew up with also went to the same Catholic church every Sunday. We went on church trips and celebrated first communion and confirmations together. I was close to my group of friends since grade school. Looking back at myself as a young child I would say that I was a quiet, shy, polite, and happy kid. Our weekends were filled with sleepovers or going to the movies and shopping at the mall. We lived in an area where everyone knew everyone. Our doors were kept unlocked and we played for hours out in the woods.

My best friend's parents owned a pizza shop in the next small town up from where I lived. It was our sophomore year in high school and during math class one day, she started having horrifically bad headaches. Alessia was unable to play soccer because of way the headaches affected her balance. Soon she started missing school. It did not seem like much at the time, we were only fifteen years old.

It was a Saturday when I came home from shopping with my parents and there was a voicemail left on the answering machine. We pressed play and Alessia left a message saying that she was at the hospital, they found a tumor in her brain. I called her back right away and she explained that she would have to have surgery. After getting off the phone, I was not sure what a tumor was. *Was it something they just quickly cut out of her head?* Nothing made sense to me.

The day of her surgery, my family met her and her family at the hospital. When we arrived Alessia, her brother, and I went down to the cafeteria and had ice cream. It was a vanilla soft serve ice cream, where you could add as many sprinkles and toppings as you wanted. She didn't seem afraid and told me everything would be okay. I didn't understand what a brain tumor was, I just thought that they would take it out and everything would go right back to normal. Because Alessia didn't seem scared at all, it made me feel less afraid. Looking back now, I believe she was the bravest person I have ever known.

I could see the fear and worry in her parents' faces. We were so young, and it is true that youth does not fear anything at all. She went into surgery, and we were all there afterwards. Alessia was in a wheelchair and another one of our friends was present too. We took Alessia off the floor to get her out of her room. There was something different about her. Soon Alessia got stronger after a lot of physical therapy, and she could walk on her own. She had occupational and physical therapists who would come to her home to collaborate with her to help her get stronger. She had teachers come also to make sure she did not fall behind in school. But there was something off that I did not understand until I became a nurse. She was off school for so long that I felt like she had a fear of going back. She would tell me constantly that she was not the same person that she was before.

She had outbursts of becoming very emotional or very mean towards me and others. I knew that she could not help it but sometimes it hurt my feelings. *Did something happen during surgery?* Soon she did come back to school, but it was only for a day. She came for lunch. It was great having her back at school since I was so lonely without my best friend. I continued to go to her house after school to visit.

Alessia and her mom planned her sixteenth birthday party in July, which was a huge family and friends celebration of her overcoming her brain tumor. It was as big as a wedding. She had a beautiful pinkish purple dress with a sparkly tiara. All our friends from school were there. We danced and ate tons of delicious food. It was held at the Hotel Hershey which was an incredibly special place that usually held fancy weddings and parties. She seemed so happy that day. This was the beginning of her life again. After having the surgery and recovery she was becoming herself again. This was just a big bump in the road.

Slowly as the weeks went by, she began to have more headaches and weaknesses. She had a tough time walking and using the left side of her body. Each time I went to visit her after school she was getting worse. I had my driver's license and more freedom, so my friend and I decided to go together to visit with her. We knocked on the back door and next to the door were about ten or twenty oxygen tanks lined up. Alessia's mom answered the door, and we walked back to her bedroom.

Alessia was laying on her couch in her bedroom. Her eyes were closed, and her mother hugged me and started crying. I did not understand what was happening. I thought she was just having a difficult day and would soon recover again. She had oxygen tubing running through her nose with a big tank next to the couch. She could not even open her eyes, but she could hear us talking. If you asked her yes or no questions, she would scrunch her eyes, so you knew she was still able to answer. I kissed her on the cheek, and we left.

A few days later I was going downstairs to eat lunch in my high school cafeteria. My friend—that was with me when I last visited—stopped me to tell me that she just heard that Alessia had passed away. Not one of my teachers told me what had happened. Our high school was a small class of about two hundred kids, so the news spread quickly.

About a week before she passed away, one of my history teachers had stopped me in the hallway and told me that I needed to go visit Alessia. It makes sense to me today why he was so stern with me to go visit her. This shocked me, and I could not believe it. I ran upstairs and called my mom, and she picked me up from school. As soon as I got home, I ran up to my room and cried. I cannot remember anything about the rest of the day. My mom told me that someone had called in the middle of the night but when she answered no one spoke. I believe it was Alessia calling to let us know that she made it over to the other side.

My family and I went to her viewing where they played a video of her with a series of beautiful pictures. "Brown-Eyed Girl" played in the background. We hugged and cried with her family, and I kissed her goodbye. I never saw a deceased person before. Why did it have to be my best friend? I knew then that my calling in life was to help others.

Weeks after her passing, reality hit that my best friend was gone and I slipped into a deep depression. I did not bounce back from grieving like everyone else around me did. I was so depressed that I no longer wanted to live. I had suicidal ideations and attempted to carry them out, more than once. One of my sister's classmates had hung herself with a belt by placing it between the top of her bedroom door and closing it. I tried to copy her idea, but I became scared and told my parents. For my junior and senior year of high school I was in and out of psychiatric treatment centers. If I felt any type of stress, I automatically had suicidal thoughts. During an afternoon when my mom was downstairs, I ingested a handful of my antidepressant medications and a mixture of my dad's medications. I started to feel drowsy and was starting to hallucinate. I remember seeing fish and snakes floating around and the walls looked like they were cracking. I laid down in my parent's bed and yelled for my mom to come. She ran up the stairs and I told her what I took.

While she was frantically on the phone, I remember I had an out of body experience. This is a sensation of your consciousness leaving your body. These are often reported by people who've had a near-death experience. During this experience I had a feeling of floating and could see myself lying in my bed and my mom at the bottom of the bed. My mom was on the phone calling our next-door neighbor to come over and then called an ambulance. She later told me that there were two large EMT males who came to take me to the hospital and that I was not cooperating, and I had punched one of them. She said that they were not expecting a small young girl to be so strong. They gave me something so I wouldn't be combative. She told me that I was taken to the Harrisburg hospital and given activated charcoal to help more rapidly remove the drugs from my body.

Once I was medically stable, they transferred me to an inpatient psychiatric facility. It was also the birth time of antidepressants hitting the shelves for the treatment of depression. It seemed like if one drug did not cure my depression, we tried another. From moving off one drug and onto another quickly, I had suffered from side effects. I ended up totaling my car near my home on a drive to my friend's house. I do not remember that day clearly at all. Luckily, I only suffered a bad concussion but was hospitalized again because professionals' feared it was a suicide attempt.

With the help of therapy and finding the right medication to treat my depression, I managed to graduate high school. I had a teacher who came to my house. She was my brother's friend's mom and she worked extra hard with me to make sure that I passed my last class to graduate. During that time, I didn't care about school. Looking back, I probably would have just dropped out if my parents had let me. She didn't give up on me and I am very thankful for that. My friends tried to help me as much as they could. But we were children, and they didn't know how.

After graduating from high school, my friend Mia and I decided not to go to college right away, and instead rented out an apartment. Mia was extremely outgoing and had all kinds of different friends, she always saw the good in everyone no matter what their past held. She never judged others and treated everyone equally. With her beautiful long black hair and huge infectious smile, she could make any dreadful day better. During those years, I was never interested in dating. I had a few flings here and there but never anything serious. At that time, dating continued to be something that was not on my radar. I had to figure out how to live on my own. My parents were still helping me out with my rent payments and a car, so I decided to take a two-week course on becoming a nurse's aide. I enjoyed helping others and felt it would be a good start.

The following summer, Mia drove out to Harrisburg to look for a job. She came back so happy that she landed a server job at this cute little Italian restaurant. She said it was nice and that the owner made all the food himself. She said all the seafood, meats, fruits, vegetables, and desserts were all brought in from a place in Philadelphia, and that every dish was sautéed separately and cooked special to order. She shared that she was making generous tips and was happy.

One night they were short with help at the restaurant. She asked me if I wanted to come help clean tables and run food. I was not doing anything, so I said I could. It was one of the few times I was in the city of Harrisburg.

I hated the city and never had a desire to go there. We parked a few blocks from the restaurant and walked from there. Parked in front of the restaurant was a black shiny Hummer truck with chrome rims and a large roof rack.

It must be the owner's truck, I thought.

The restaurant was small fine dining, I could smell garlic in the air as soon as we opened the door. We walked in and I saw small wooden upholstered chairs with fresh linen covered tables set close to each other; it seemed very intimate and looked like a lovely place to go on a date. The tables were set perfectly with sparkling wine glasses, white folded napkins, and shiny silverware. More wine glasses hung from a mini coffee bar in the back and the coffee bar had large antique copper and brass coffee machines. There was a red Victorian couch with carved wooden flowers painted gold against the back wall and Frank Sinatra music played softly in the background.

I followed Mia to the back of the restaurant through a swinging kitchen door where I met a young dark-haired Italian man who turned around from sautéing a chicken dish. He smiled and introduced himself as Mr. S. Later, I learned his name was Anthony. The kitchen was extremely small and very hot. It was probably about a ten-by-ten-foot room. As soon as you walked in there was a large stainless steel double fridge to your right and two prep stations with gas stoves in the back and a sink and dishwasher in the corner. You were literally working right up against each other. He was incredibly happy that Mia had brought me there to help. My job that night was to clean tables, deliver food, and keep the customers happy.

The restaurant was packed that evening. It was only a weeknight and there wasn't a single empty seat. That night was my first experience ever working in a restaurant. Mr. S. kept smiling and having small conversations with me. He asked me where I was from, what my hobbies were, and what I liked to do for fun. At the end, he thanked me for helping him out and paid me a hundred dollars for working about five hours. I had never made that much money in one day before then, so I told him if he ever needed help again to just ask.

A few days later, Mia returned to our apartment after her shift and asked if I wanted to go hang out with Anthony. He picked us up that evening in the Hummer and drove us to his friend's strip club. I remember thinking it was an odd place to take two eighteen-year-olds, but we went with it anyway. Everything he spoke about sounded amazing and new to me. I had never met anyone like him; he was so well groomed and wore an Armani shirt.

We arrived at the club hearing music blasting. The man at the door knew Anthony and introduced himself to Mia and me as Matt. He was huge and looked like a bodyguard. When we walked in, we saw topless girls everywhere, I was surprised to see that many weren't very pretty. One of the girls on stage was pregnant. They came up to us, asking if we wanted lap dances. Mia and I just looked at each other and giggled nervously. We sat down in front of the stage and Anthony gave us dollar bills to give to the strippers. To us, at the time, it all seemed like innocent fun.

Anthony introduced us to the owner of the club, Mark, who was also his friend. He looked Italian—with the same dark hair and handsome smile as Anthony—and around the same age. They asked if we wanted to go back to Mark's house, behind the strip club. It all still seemed very innocent to us.

His house was a huge bachelor pad. There were multiple large fish tanks with tropical fish, mirrors everywhere, and neon lighting. We started drinking and playing a card game, and we were laughing and having a good time. As it grew late, Mark took Mia back to his bedroom, and I went into a back bedroom with Anthony. Things started to move quickly after our first kiss.

"No, I'm not like that," I said. He respected me and stopped. I felt safe and in control that evening. The next morning, Anthony dropped Mia and I back off at our apartment. Before I got out of the truck, I looked him in the eyes and squeezed his hand, thanking him for taking me out. He smiled back. Later that night he started calling to ask what I was doing. He was very charming and sweet.

Mia thought our age difference of twelve years was strange because Anthony was an older man, but I didn't think it mattered. I had never felt like that about anyone before. He gave me butterflies.

··· Chapter Two

If someone had asked me, at the age of eighteen, if I would stay in an abusive relationship, I would've said, "No way!" What I didn't know then is that this is never how the relationship starts. Abuse slowly seeps in, until one day you look back and wonder how it all started—how it got so bad.

When I first met Anthony, he was sweet and charming. He was interested in my life; where I grew up and went to school. He would leave the restaurant just to see me. It made me feel important when he would put his busy life on hold just for me.

After all, you put your life on hold and make sacrifices for people you really like, right?

Anthony was smart and funny. He created the illusion that I set the pace of our relationship, that I made the decisions. In the beginning, he adored me. He asked about my dreams and what I wanted to do with my life. He let me pick the places where we would eat. He took me shopping and bought art supplies because he knew I loved to paint. He asked me what we should do on the weekends. I felt like I had opinions and choices in our new and exciting relationship. It seemed like a magical trust that we had together.

He shared a story that he'd never told before, about an unbelievably bad accident that he was in. He told me that once when he was alone, he stepped out of his tow truck and tripped and broke his leg. And that he was so embarrassed, he purposely wrecked his truck down the side of a hill to make it look like he had been in an accident. I felt special because he trusted me to tell his secrets to. I also shared with Anthony about my past and how my best friend in high school had recently passed away. A spark in his eyes went off and he joyfully said that he worked in Alessia's parents' pizza shop as a teenager. He told me that Alessia's mother was his aunt, which made me feel like we were brought together for a reason.

When it was time for my parents to meet Anthony, he thought it would be a great idea to invite them to the restaurant and treat them to a delicious meal. That night, I noticed an older woman working for Anthony who I had never met. She was very skinny and looked about thirty-five with short, messy brown hair. Her face was long, and she looked exhausted with bags under her eyes. I ordered pasta carbonara, which Anthony made special for me earlier that week, and it was so delicious that I wanted it again. Anthony came over to our table after she brought our food out, but only stopped to talk to my parents for a brief minute. He was noticeably short and a bit rude, which was unlike how I had ever seen him before. The restaurant wasn't even busy. After we finished eating, the server brought the check out. Minutes later, Anthony came to the table, pointing out that he took fifty percent off the bill.

My parents paid the bill but were clearly shocked to have received a bill at all. Their first impressions on Anthony were that they straight forward did not like him. My mom felt that he was sketchy and acted like a "know-it-all." My mom said that he had signs of a predator including turning on the charm and she thought to herself what would a twenty-nine-year-old want to do with an eighteen-year-old who just graduated high school? My parents were both concerned because in their gut, they didn't trust Anthony. But since I was now an adult, they knew that I was able to make my own decisions. They didn't want to scare me away because I was fragile, after just healing from my deep depression. In my mind, this was the best thing that had happened to me; Anthony was my first boyfriend. Today, I look back and realize that if my parents would have told me to get away from Anthony, and that he was no good, I would have shut them out. It's like my parents knew that he would eventually hurt me, and they wanted to keep the door open.

Anthony often bragged about the large boat he kept docked down in Delaware Beach. He said he wanted to take Mia and I out on it before he had to winterize and store it away. It was a warm day in September, and we all drove down to the beach together in Anthony's Hummer. I had never been on a private boat before. When we arrived at the beach, Anthony stopped at the liquor store and bought a case of wine coolers. We parked the truck in the marina parking lot and walked down to the docks with our overnight bags. Since we were underage, we could not go to the bar next to the marina, so we started drinking on the boat.

    It had been a beautiful sunny day. His boat was a yacht, with two bedrooms, a small kitchen and bathroom. Anthony started it up and we took it out onto the ocean. He even let me drive. It had felt surreal to be out on the ocean in a yacht owned by my boyfriend. Later, we took the boat back to the dock and got ready for the evening. We were all feeling tipsy from drinking wine coolers. Anthony suggested we play a card game, like "Truth or Dare," and he tried to get Mia and I naked. It seemed like he was trying to get us both to have sex with him, but Mia stopped and went to her bedroom.

    Anthony and I did sleep together that night. He seemed upset and I didn't want him to be mad, so I did whatever he asked. The next morning, we all got up and cleaned the boat and traveled back home. It was a silent car ride; the fun was clearly over. We stopped for lunch at a Fuddruckers and when the bill arrived, he made Mia pay for her own meal. That seemed odd. It was like he was punishing her for not doing what he wanted her to do the night before.

"I have to tell you something," Mia said, after we returned to our apartment.

She explained that on her first night working for Anthony, he was there with her and another employee as they were closing the restaurant. She was about to leave but Anthony had stopped her and talked her into having a drink at the bar with him and the other young girl. Mia said she had a few shots and that Anthony had gotten them both drunk and dared them both to kiss. Mia admitted that she kissed the other girl. At the time they were underage. Mia said that was all that happened. I approached Anthony the next day and asked him about it, but he shrugged it off like it was no big deal. He told me it was just a joke. So, I thought nothing of it.

A few months after Mia and I had been living together in our apartment, she began to bring random new friends she had just met at the local coffee shop over to hang out. I never had any problems with it, they were nice. One night I was upstairs studying for my nurse's aide class when I heard a loud knocking on the back door. Our apartment was above a jewelry store, so you had to walk upstairs in the back of the building to enter. I was not expecting anyone, and the knocking kept going. I peeked my head around the corner of the kitchen, so whoever it was that they would not see me. It was a tall guy from the coffee shop. I never talked to him and decided to just ignore his knocking because no one else was home and I was not going to let a stranger into our apartment.

After about ten minutes, he was still there knocking. I decided to call Anthony because I was getting scared because this guy wasn't leaving. I should have called Mia and asked her if she was expecting someone. Again, Anthony made me feel incredibly special, because without asking him to come over he was at my apartment within five minutes. I heard Anthony screaming at the guy, telling him to leave. I could hear the other man asking to talk to Mia, but Anthony scared him so he finally left. I felt like he saved the day. After this happened, Anthony suggested that I should come live with him. He said that I was not safe living there. He was about to sign a lease to rent a house north of Harrisburg. Within a few days, I was packed up and moving into a house with him. I left my apartment in such a rush that I did not even discuss it with Mia.

"It is extremely dangerous for you to live there with Mia," he said. And I believed him. Anthony convinced my parents that Mia was a drug addict and that all kinds of strange people were in and out of our apartment. He painted a picture that she was a horrible influence, that she did drugs, and I should not be around people like that. Soon, Mia no longer worked at his restaurant either. A friendship that I had for years disappeared; he made her vanish from my life. Just like that.

The house Anthony and I later moved into was a small two-story white house with green shutters and a nice front porch and detached garage. It had a big yard that sat out towards the woods. There were a few other neighbors that lived down our lane. With all the bragging he did, you would have thought Anthony was a millionaire, but the house was just a small basic rental. I helped Anthony move all his furniture from storage units into the house. Again, I felt special because this was *our* house. Our relationship had moved at an extremely fast pace in a few short months, but it was my first relationship and felt like a fairy tale.

We decorated the house together. He let me choose where to put up the new pictures and decorations. We went shopping and picked out brand new sheets, comforters, towels, shower curtains, pictures, and dishes together. Everything in the house was brand new. In the bedroom, he spent an hour showing me exactly how he wanted his clothes folded or hung. His dress pants and shirts had to be in a color-coded order hung up in the closet by wooden hangers only. His socks and underwear had to be folded and placed very neatly in the drawers. His dress ties had to be hung up on a special rack and jewelry placed on his dresser laid out. The rest of the house had to be just as spotless. I was only allowed a tiny closet in the spare room, where I had to keep all my belongings. I remember being confused, but quickly brushed it off thinking there wasn't a lot of closet space in our bedroom.

We went to pick up more of Anthony's items at another house, where a lady stepped out to greet us. I quickly realized it was the same woman that was the server the night my parents came to Anthony's restaurant. She questioned Anthony about why I was with him.

"Oh Betty, she's just helping me move," he said, casually.

"Okay," Betty scoffed before stomping back into her house with disgust.

I asked Anthony why she acted that way, and he brushed it off like it was nothing to worry about. So, I didn't worry and continued helping him load up the rest of his stuff. I began to notice Anthony's collection of guns and asked why he had so many.

"For protection," he shrugged.

Even though I didn't know it at the time, the threat of violence was already there inside that house that we had just made our first home together.

Once we were settled, I decided that I wanted to continue my education by attending the community college that was ten minutes away from our house. My parents paid for my first semester, and I was enrolled to begin my pre-requisite classes for nursing to become a Registered Nurse. I attended school full-time and went straight to work at the restaurant until it closed every single night. I found myself falling asleep during lectures, I forgot to complete homework and do assigned reading. I failed exams. My first semester, I only passed one class. I was unable to study because I was working so much. But Anthony said that I had to work full time for him. He said that working for him was how I held up my half of the rent. But he never paid me when I worked at the restaurant, instead he said that if I wanted or needed something all I had to do was ask.

After my first college semester ended, and I failed all my classes but one, my parents said they would not pay for another semester. I decided to stop school and just work for Anthony. I was working so much that I slowly stopped calling and seeing my parents. Before I knew it, the only people I talked to was Anthony and the others who worked at the restaurant. With working all the time for Anthony, I had no time for my friends, and they all slowly started to disappear. I thought that I should be helping Anthony at the restaurant because the people he hired usually quit or were fired every few weeks. I believed that people who love each other help each other out.

Anthony made it clear to me not to share my personal life that we had together with the other people who worked in the restaurant. He said, "You are here to work not to socialize, and I do not want anyone knowing my personal life." I listened to him and did as I was told. He was now in control of my body. He told me that I was overweight and fat. He had me working so much and barely eating that I lost weight. Then he would tell me I was too skinny, and it was disgusting. Suddenly, I was never good enough for him.

Coercive control is the strategic form of ongoing psychological and emotional abuse that is based on control, manipulation, and oppression. I can see today that coercive control was associated with Anthony's narcissism-fueled abuse. I was so damaged that I never recognized I was being controlled and manipulated, because my self-esteem, sense of safety, and autonomy had become undone. My autonomy was limited by Anthony restricting my use of a car, devaluing my choice of friends, and taking my phone from time to time away from me. What makes coercive control so dangerous is that it comes off as Anthony trying to "save me." He became the "hero" because he kept me away from my "bad" friends. The goal was to keep me reliant on him financially, emotionally, and psychologically, so that my autonomy would be limited.

There was a small quiet young girl who worked on and off again at the restaurant; her name was Vicki. She was petite with long brown hair and a dark complexion. She only worked in the kitchen and helped cook. She was very pretty but not too social, she only seemed to interact with Anthony. When he asked her to do something she jumped for him at the snap of his fingers. You could tell that there was something going on between the two of them. It was obvious that they had once had a relationship together. Whenever I was at the restaurant when Vicki or Betty worked, I was treated like just another worker and not Anthony's girlfriend. I soon found out that Anthony did indeed have relationships with both Vicki and Betty. Shockingly all three of us were working together in that small restaurant, but none of us knew about the other that had dated Anthony for some time. He had managed to maintain control of all three of us at the same time.

Friday nights were one of the busiest nights for the restaurant. Anthony's mom would come and help as a hostess. The first time I met her, Betty, Vicki, and I were all working. She walked in and was about five feet tall and looked like she weighed about four hundred pounds. She smiled and was very polite and nice to me. When she spoke, she talked in a baby voice and acted innocent. Her role was to seat the customers and help clear tables. She drove an hour every Friday night to come, and the following Friday I understood why.

Anthony had a ten-year-old daughter named Mickey. He did not tell me about her until she stayed with us one weekend. She had light brown hair cut in a bob that sat above her shoulders and a big smile with a mouthful of braces. She was not timid and talked to anyone. Anthony's mom began to stay at our house on the weekends Mickey was with us. It was not until later that I understood he had been court ordered for supervised visits with his daughter. At the time, I thought they were a happy family spending time together. Little did I know Anthony's mom came because he paid her.

Anthony had Mickey work in the restaurant every weekend she stayed with us. For a typical ten-year-old this was not fun for her. Anthony more frequently had a temper while he worked in the back of the restaurant. When we were short staffed, he begged Vicki to come into work. If she was not able to work, he became mean to everyone around him because he had to cook by himself. She was the only other person who knew exactly how to cook like he did. She had been carefully trained, so he didn't trust anyone else to cook.

I could tell when Anthony was flirting with Vicki in the back of the kitchen because they would secretly be laughing to their own jokes. When I walked into the kitchen one evening, they instantly stopped talking. I ignored it all because I was so exhausted all the time and did not want to feel jealous. Vicki did not know that I was living with Anthony. She needed a ride to work one day, and they stopped by our house when I was not around. She used the only bathroom that was located upstairs and saw that there was shampoo for blonde hair in the bathtub. She instantly became angry at Anthony and would not work that evening. The next time she saw me in the restaurant she questioned me whether I was living with Anthony, and I confirmed that I was. She thought that I was just his roommate, not his girlfriend. I listened to Anthony and did not discuss our personal life with anyone else. Even though I believed he was being unfaithful, I still respected him and his requests.

It was a busy Friday one night, and Anthony and Vicki were returning from picking up food for the weekend in Philadelphia. It was one of the events they did together while I prepped the food for the night and made pasta sauce after the lunch crowd. They came back with fresh shrimp, calamari, clams, mussels, and veal. When they arrived back to the restaurant Anthony parked the truck and we unloaded everything from the back alley. A few minutes later Betty arrived. She did not look happy to be working again. Instantly, she started to have an argument with Anthony. I was not sure what they were fighting about but it sounded as if money was involved. As I walked towards the back of the restaurant, I saw him push her outside the back door forcefully. She did not return. I did not question Anthony about what happened. I kept my head down and walked away. That evening he screamed, yelled, and cussed at the entire staff. He could tell that I was a little scared. He smiled slightly and explained later that this is normal behavior.

"This is how all restaurant owners act in the kitchen," he told me later.

One evening Anthony's mom took me to the side.

"Anthony said the first day you worked for him you were washing dishes in the back of the restaurant and that was when he knew you were the one for him," she said.

Hearing that from her made me feel special. She soon made remarks about Betty too, how she had been around Anthony since before he dated Mickey's mother. She also told me that Vicki would jump as high as Anthony asked. I was so overworked and tired that this surprisingly did not bother me. It came off as gossip and I noticed that his mom loved to tell stories.

I quickly learned when working with Anthony that everything had to be done perfectly and his way; there was no room for error. The narcissistic perfectionist sets these unrealistic goals and targets for other people. They get angry and hostile if other people don't reach their impossible goals. High expectations paired with feelings of grandiosity and entitlement to the perfect performance of others creates a much more negative combination. Anthony was hyper-critical about everything I did in the restaurant. He was completely unprofessional in front of his employees and would scream at them if they made a mistake, but if Anthony messed up an order or cooked something wrong it was never his fault. He could bend the rules but no one else ever could. If I tried to explain why something went wrong, he didn't want to hear an explanation because they were excuses. If the restaurant was not clean and prepped a certain way, it was the end of the world. I noticed that he started to become short-tempered with me when speaking. If the bathrooms were not spotless or the floors were not swept well enough, he screamed and cussed at me. I felt like I had to maintain constant perfection, especially when training new people in the restaurant. Of course, I didn't want to make Anthony angry; I wanted him to know that I was working my hardest for him because I cared. I wanted to be the best girlfriend he'd ever had.

In his restaurant, I began to notice that his customers were usually people he knew. His normal lunch crowd consisted of important judges, lawyers, and law makers. Anthony bragged about how he knew all these important people and how much of a big deal it was to him. If there was a homeless man or person who looked like they were on drugs outside the restaurant, he had the police there within minutes to remove them. After we closed for a few hours between the lunch and dinner shift, the local police would sometimes come down and I would have to cook lunches for them by myself. Anthony knew a lot of important people, or made it appear that way.

Anthony always took great fascination in looking his best and having the best cars, clothes, and jewelry. Narcissists enjoy looking at themselves in the mirror. They may spend more time grooming themselves to boost their grandiose self-images. Anthony used to tell me that he looked like a movie star and deserved to be an actor. A key trait that Anthony held was confidence because he believed in his own attractiveness. The city of Harrisburg had an art show every year where they closed off the front street of the city along the river. Only knowing Anthony for a few months, he bought me a thousand-dollar watermelon stone bracelet from Madagascar. I felt extremely special when he bought this for me, it was my first piece of real jewelry. It was a beautiful bracelet with gold, silver, and pink stones that looked like watermelon slices. His mom was there that weekend and she was quite impressed as well. But just like everything he ever bought me, he also took it back. It was never really mine in the first place. When he got angry with me, I had to take the bracelet off and give it back to him.

On my nineteenth birthday, Anthony surprised me with a puppy, a grey Sicilian mastiff—also called a Cane Corso—with a white dot on his chest and white toes. We named him Ferelli. His cousin from Italy did not want this puppy so he bought it for me, which had felt like a big new chapter in our relationship. I told Anthony that I loved him when he gave the puppy to me. His response was, "No, you don't love me, you love the puppy."

We brought Ferelli to my parent's house to show them that weekend.

Anthony was extremely strict and controlling with Ferelli; he would not allow him to have any toys or treats, only dog food. Anthony said that I could only show him so much love and affection. I thought that was mean and odd, but Anthony said he was training him so I did not continue to question it.

We had Anthony's family over to our house later that month to meet the puppy. His mom, daughter, and brother came over for dinner. The weirdest thing about that day was when Betty walked through the door. *Why was Betty invited to come over?* Looking back now, she never knew that I was Anthony's girlfriend. She walked right in like she was there before. She did know that I was living with Anthony but that I was only his roommate. She conversed with his family and had a wonderful time but didn't say "hi" to me once. Soon everyone left and I felt oddly intrigued by what had just happened but brushed it off anyway. When I first met Anthony, he asked if I was a jealous girl and I had answered no.

During Friday and Saturday nights, after we closed the restaurant, we usually went downtown to the other bars and hung out with Anthony's friends. We went out several times with his friend Mark—who I learned grew up with Anthony—and his friends. Mark seemed to have a different girl on his arm every night, but even so, they were all hilarious and fun to go hang out with. We walked into all the bars and got served like we were special VIPs. This went on for a few months, until Anthony began to send me home by myself and come home late, if at all. One night I received a phone call extremely late from him to say he had wrecked his truck under the bridge near the restaurant. He said he was okay but was at Betty's house. *Why was he with Betty?* He said Betty was a longtime good friend of his and not to worry. Anthony eventually came home the next day, after Betty dropped him off in the afternoon.

The next day I learned that his truck wasn't in his name, it was in Vicki's. *Why would he have his own vehicle in another person's name?* Then, I learned he didn't have insurance on it, and because of that, Vicki lost her license. Anthony had to find another vehicle and was obligated to drive Vicki wherever she pleased. It was strange to me that everything

Anthony "owned" wasn't in his name. The house and restaurant utilities, phone bills, and vehicles were either in Vicki's or Betty's names.

Regardless of the red flags that were clearly revealing themselves, I was still unable to see them. Instead, I felt that my relationship with Anthony was going well because I didn't have another relationship to compare it to. As a restaurant owner, he was always busy. I empathized with this and excused his anger and constant frustration with others. It seemed his employees never stayed long, so he was constantly replacing staff.

"This is the way the restaurant business goes," he would say. "Employees will come and go and are usually never dependable."

And so, I tried to make his life as smooth as possible, which meant that most days I was the one running the restaurant by myself. Being as young as I was, it was a huge responsibility.

One extremely hot summer night, I was alone at our house with Mickey. We had gotten home late; I had worked a long night at the restaurant. I made sure she was tucked in and said goodnight. I turned the window air conditioner unit on upstairs in our bedrooms and shut the doors. I was so exhausted that I fell asleep as soon as my head hit the pillow. But was later woken abruptly to hands tightly gripping my neck.

···· Chapter Three

"You stupid bitch!" Anthony yelled. "What the fuck, you locked me out of the house! Don't you dare scream, Mickey is sleeping, I will knock you out!"

Was I dreaming?

He pushed me down back into the bed and shoved my face into a pillow. I could not breathe for what felt like forever until he let go of my head, got up, and left the room. I could hear him downstairs stomping his feet until eventually he fell asleep on the couch. I was wide awake but didn't make a sound. Mickey was in the bedroom beside ours and I was hoping she was still asleep. I trembled in my bed alone, wondering what had just happened.

I wasn't even able to say that I was sorry.

Immediately after, I felt confused as to why that just happened. I instantly felt a ray of emotions ranging from anxiety, shame, fear, powerlessness, and guilt. Being left alone in that state of mind made me feel rejected, and my self-esteem and psychological health were becoming damaged.

The following morning, I got up, took a shower, and walked downstairs slowly on eggshells fearing for how he was going to act. Anthony was still sleeping on the couch. He slowly woke up and told me to come over to him and lay on the couch. He kissed my forehead and told me he was sorry about last night.

"Just make sure it does not happen again," he said. "I had to break in through a window."

It was *my* fault that he didn't have a key. It was *my* fault the window now needed to be fixed. It was embarrassing for *him* that the neighbors across the street may have heard him pounding hard on his own front door. This was the first time Anthony physically hurt me. This was the beginning of me going through the cycle of abuse. It started with the "tension building phase" that consisted of Anthony lashing out in anger for being locked out of the house. Second, the "incident of abuse phase" was waking up to hands tightly choking my throat, insults, name calling, and more physical violence. Third, after the tension fades is the reconciliation. Anthony kissed my forehead as a loving gesture to move us into the "reconciliation phase." Last, the "calm phase" is where we both come up with some sort of explanation or justification for what has happened. For me I knew that I won't ever let Anthony get locked out again. This cycle of abuse defined our relationship and continued on repeat.

Narcissists will compartmentalize people in their lives. They like to separate their friends from their family, and their partners from their colleagues. I realize today that Anthony dramatically changed, depending on who was around him. If he wanted or needed something, he was sweet and charming. But if I did something wrong, it was like a switch flipping and he would cuss and scream at me for the slightest situation. Keeping people apart, especially Anthony's many girlfriends, helped him lead multiple lives. Narcissists don't know who they really are. He was prepared to paint different pictures for people to get what he wanted. Anthony couldn't fully control others to keep their secrets, but he could maintain control by keeping you away from them. Anthony wanted to keep our relationship quiet because at one time, I was the affair. Anthony kept his exes around for an ego boost. He was rarely done with someone when they split up. He portrayed himself as single, helping create the illusion that he was available. In his mind it kept his exes hungry for him and eager to please. Secrecy was another dynamic involved in this cycle of abuse I was enduring. Both Anthony and I were keeping our relationship a secret, he told me to never discuss our personal life with anyone. He said that it is completely normal for couples to get into fights and for the husband or man in the relationship to hit his wife or girlfriend. He explained that every relationship is exactly like this, and that this is very normal for couples to experience.

"I'm positive even your dad hits your mom sometimes," he said.

I *still* believed him.

We continued that Sunday with Mickey, like every other Sundays. As though what had happened never happened. We usually went to visit his mom, unless she was already over. He no longer had to do supervised visits. When Mickey's mom dropped her off, I always got a sense from her that she thought to herself, "Good luck with that man." Mickey's mom was well put together—she had a good job, her own house and most importantly, she was a good strong and loving mother to Mickey. She was never mean towards me, but something was not right. I sensed from her that their relationship had a painful past and her current interactions with Anthony were short and filled with pure disgust.

Looking back today, I realize that we have a lot in common.

The first few months Anthony and I dated, we spent the holidays with my family. When we went to holiday dinners, he was always the star of the conversations. He tried to wow and impress everyone with his stories and successes. He made sure the car that he was driving that day was sparkling, and his Rolex and diamond rings were flashy. He wore expensive designer clothing, while I had to shop at discount stores or keep wearing my restaurant clothes.

Driving back from shopping one day, Anthony and I got into an argument in the car. To this day, I cannot remember exactly what it was about; it wasn't about anything significant or important. If I did not know the exact facts about something I did or something that happened, I was a liar. There was no time to think or process what he was asking me. These arguments became more frequent and daily now. But leaving him still never crossed my mind. I wanted to fix the problem so the fighting would end.

When we got into arguments, if I "talked back," Anthony had started to slap me in the head or face. His big diamond ring hurt the most. When he was driving, and I was not paying attention, he would hit me for no reason. One time he hit me so hard that my head bounced off the passenger side window. I was backhanded in the nose so hard that blood started pouring out. My nose did not break that time, but it sure felt it had. Blood splattered everywhere—all over the middle console and on my seat. Anthony pulled over and hurried to clean the car. And it was my fault. Again, we went through the cycle of abuse. Over time, the "reconciliation phase" started to fade out. This happened once Anthony started to feel more in control of our relationship.

Before I began dating Anthony, I was seeing a therapist and taking antidepressants to treat my depression. But a few months into our relationship, he told me to stop taking them.

"You do not need to go to counseling," he had said. "This depression is your own choice."

He took my antidepressant medications and flushed them down the toilet. Soon after I started suffering from side effects after stopping my medications abruptly. I had never felt so sick; I had horrible nausea, vomiting, chills, and shakes. I knew I still needed counseling, but he said that I was "choosing" to be sad.

"Stop with your bullshit and get over it or I will chain you up in the basement." Anthony yelled at me one day.

He laughed and bragged about how he chained his own brother up in a basement because he was going through a bad divorce and was depressed. Anthony said his brother was so depressed that he wanted to kill himself. He did get proper help eventually, but Anthony said he had to try to take control into his own hands. Again, I'll never know if he made this story up or if it really happened. It was around this time that I stopped talking to my family; he made me believe my parents were bad people who wanted to keep me on antidepressant medications so they could keep full control of my life. I was tired from working so much that I was not able to process and heal from my depression, much less what was really going on during this time. My parents tried to call to check up on me, but Anthony took my phone. He wouldn't let me talk to my friends either.

I woke up early every morning to drive to the restaurant by myself. When I arrived, I propped open the doors to carry out a large outdoor rug to unroll onto the sidewalk. I carried out huge cement planter pots, filled with flowers and dirt, to place them in rows lining the edges of the rug. I carried out tables and chairs to set up the outdoor seating section. I rolled out the awning that covered the seating. And I rolled out another rug with the restaurant name on it. After setting up the outside, I came in and mopped the floors and started cooking the pasta and sauce. A few hours later, Anthony arrived only minutes before we opened for lunch. After lunch, Anthony usually left and went somewhere without telling me where he was going. I was left alone at the restaurant for a few hours and sometimes became so tired that I took a nap behind the counter on the cold floor. I later prepared for dinner and worked until closing, which was normally ten or eleven at night during the weekdays and even later Friday and Saturday nights. I cleaned up and washed all the lunch and dinner dishes because it was rare that Anthony had a dishwasher. And I never received a single paycheck.

I ask myself today, "Was I the victim of labor trafficking?" This is a crime that involves compelling or coercing a person to provide labor or services and affects persons of all ages, races, genders, and nationalities.

Labor traffickers often prey on those with vulnerable life circumstances and economic hardships. I was young, naïve, and had major depression. I was perfect prey for Anthony.

Working so many hours every day consumed my life. Yes, I had a schedule, but I soon had no control of my daily activities. My days consisted of going to work, sleeping, and going back to work. And I never saw a penny. The only time Anthony paid me was the first night that I worked for him. He made me feel extremely guilty if I asked him for new clothes.

"Your clothes are fine and if you want something new it must be for the restaurant only," he would say.

I couldn't go shopping when I wanted or buy what I liked. Anthony took me to the cheapest stores and made a huge deal when he had to buy me something. Even though he always bought the best for himself. His suites were Italian tailor-made and hand-stitched. His dress shoes were always shiny and new. His hair was cut and styled at the most expensive salons, where mine was cut once a year. I weighed maybe one hundred pounds, soaking wet, and was just tired all the time.

Anthony convinced me to play card games with Vicki after work. He made us alcoholic drinks at the coffee bar after the restaurant was closed. We had gotten so drunk that Anthony drove us back to our house. There we resumed to drink. Anthony had us play a truth or dare game that always turned into him having sex with both of us. I was aware of what was happening but was too afraid to do anything but listen to him. Little did I know this would go on for over a decade.

One weeknight, as we were opening the restaurant for dinner, I was standing behind the coffee bar when Betty walked in through the doors. I was feeling a little spunky, so I decided to say something to her.

"Betty, you know Anthony and I are dating, right?" I asked. "Because I don't want anything to be weird between us, since you're good friends with him."

She took one look at me and turned bright red, for a moment I thought she was going to punch me in the face.

"Anthony just screwed me last night!" she yelled before turning around and stomping outside. I stood there shocked and disgusted.

Anthony was sitting out front at one of the outdoor tables talking on his phone and drinking wine. Betty stood in front of him, and after about fifteen minutes of yelling, she left. Anthony walked back in and even though I was mad at him, I froze in fear and stood facing him behind the bar. He did not look happy.

"You ruined my life and as a result I'm going to lose the restaurant!" he yelled.

This was all going to be my fault. He made me feel as if the restaurant he worked so hard for was now going to be shut down because of me. I felt extremely guilty when I should have felt mad at him for cheating. Anthony continued to explain that Betty had helped him start up the restaurant. She took a loan out to get it running and had all the utilities in her name. I later learned that Anthony had her working at the restaurant, but rarely paid her too. He was living with her before we moved into our house together, but still had her wishing and believing there was still something between then. A few days later, Betty was back and happy again; like the fight never happened.

And even still, the thought of leaving our relationship still never occurred to me. Anthony needed me, he loved me. He told me that I kept him feeling young and that I was good for him. He made me feel that we were a team working together. With all the bad times that I endured with Anthony, we did have some beautiful and loving memories together. Anthony took me to his cousin's wedding in Staten Island when we were first dating. He introduced me to his entire family and showed me off like he was proud of me. This made me feel good because he was introducing me to everyone as his girlfriend and telling them what a hard worker I was at his restaurant. That day we laughed, danced, held hands, and had a really good time. Moments like that made me feel like we had this great future together and I quickly put the bad times behind me. It is much more calming to remember the good times. I believe that I trained my brain to, "move on" and feel good again. Over time I can see that I started to normalize my abuse. I lowered my expectations and loosened my boundaries.

Anthony's grandmother was admitted to the hospital that following summer. I drove out to Lancaster to visit her after Anthony told me I had to. I visited her for a few hours. It was a nice visit, and I could tell she was happy to see me. She asked where Anthony was and I wasn't sure how to answer, so I told her that he was busy running errands.

It took me about an hour to drive back home. Anthony and Vicki were getting out of the car when I pulled up the driveway. I wasn't sure why she was there. I went inside the house and Ferelli had pooped upstairs on the carpet. Of course, Anthony was livid. He was still a puppy and potty training, and occasionally had accidents. Anthony grabbed him and dragged him upstairs and shoved his face in the feces. He screamed, yelled, and smacked Ferelli over the head, who was shaking and scared. Then he came up to me, grabbing my arm and yelling, "Why would something like this ever happen?"

I was scared and couldn't get words to come out of my mouth. He let go and I cleaned up the mess. Vicki stood and watched from the front door. Anthony and I were supposed to go out on the river to jet ski that afternoon. To punish me, he turned to Vicki and smiled.

"Do you want to go out on the jet ski?" She agreed with a smile on her face, and they left and shut the door in my face.

Emotional withholding in relationships refers to a pattern of behavior in which one partner intentionally withholds emotional expression, affection, or communication from the other partner. When Anthony did this, it caused feelings of frustration and loneliness in me. Being callously ignored by a narcissist, who then dotes on others in front of you, can be similar in nature to being sucker-punched in the face. And that is exactly how it felt that day.

I did not have my own car and could only use one of Anthony's cars if he allowed me. We didn't have cable TV or internet. To punish me he took my phone away. I was stuck in a house alone, and I sat on the couch and cried. Ferelli sat next to me and put his head on my lap. He knew I was sad. I couldn't understand why this was happening. I went to visit his sick grandmother and he punished me for something that I had no control over. That night Anthony didn't come home. I was left in that house more often than I would like to admit. I had to make sure the house was always spotless and clean. I had to mow and upkeep the lawn. Plus, I had to run the restaurant. It was a lot of hard physical labor. I was young so I was able to keep up, but at the end of each day I was exhausted.

I was working the lunch shift when a girl walked into the restaurant that I knew from high school. I was never friends with her in school, but I knew who she was. Her name was Samantha. She was a tall skinny girl with long, straight strawberry blonde hair and freckles on her face.

"Are you hiring?" she asked, smiling.

She was working at the hardware store down the street but wasn't happy with her job. She said she desperately needed a new job. I asked Anthony and he hired her on the spot. She started working at the restaurant and told me that she also needed a place to stay. She had just broken up with her boyfriend and was no longer living with him. She didn't want to have to drive an hour to work every day to the restaurant from her parent's house. I thought it would be cool to have a friend to stay at the house, and perhaps there wouldn't be as many fights between Anthony and me. She could help with some of the cleaning too because it was starting to take a toll.

It was a busy Friday night at the restaurant and I was standing at the coffee bar making drinks. Three police officers came walking into the restaurant and asked if I was Rebecca. I told them "yes" and quickly called for Anthony to come out from the kitchen. The officer said that he had to take me to the hospital to be evaluated for my safety. Anthony told me to just go with them and that everything would be okay. I listened and was escorted into the back of a police car. The female officer who was driving turned up the music and wouldn't tell me where we were going. We soon arrived at a local emergency department, where I had to go into a room with the officer and change into nothing but a hospital gown. At the time I didn't have any bruises on my body, but I was malnourished. My ribs showed and my face was sunken in. My hair was thin, dried out, and messy. The hospital gown that I wore swallowed me whole.

"Are you depressed, or do you feel like hurting yourself or others?" a nurse asked when she walked in.

My parents must have called them! I thought, angrily.

I know today that my parents had applied for an involuntary emergency examination and treatment for me. A form must be completed by a person who believes another person needs treatment. If this person is not a physician, police officer, the County Administrator, or his delegate, he or she must request authorization or a warrant through the County Administrator. This was not something easy to obtain. My parents must have pulled strings to make this happen. The application has boxes to check off and complete.

The three boxes are as follows:

(i) The person has acted in such manner as to evidence that he/she would be unable, without care, supervision, and the continued assistance of others, to satisfy his/her need for nourishment, personal or medical care, shelter, or self-protection and safety, and that there is reasonable probability that death, serious bodily injury or serious physical debilitation would ensure within thirty days, unless adequate treatment were afforded under the act. I was severely malnourished, needed medical care for my depression, and needed safety from Anthony. But I lied to go back to my abuser.

(ii) The person has attempted suicide and there is reasonable probability of suicide unless adequate treatment is afforded under this act. I now believe when Anthony coerced me to stop taking my antidepressants for I had become more unstable and suicidal than I was before. I was clearly not mentally okay at this point. But I lied and said that I was not suicidal ... because all that mattered was Anthony.

(iii) The person has substantially mutilated themselves substantially and there is reasonable probability of mutilation unless adequate treatment is offered under this act. I was not harming myself, but I was harming my body by starving. Again, I lied. A person is severely mentally disabled when, as a result of mental illness, their capacity to exercise self-control, judgement, and discretion in the conduct of their affairs and social relations or to care for their personal needs is so lessened that they poses a clear and present stance of harm to others or to themself. What I didn't see at the time was my parents' love and concern. They saw Anthony for who he was, when I wasn't able to. At the time, all I could think about was getting back to Anthony; he had such a strong hold over me. When I was away from him and our home, panic ran through my blood.

Several nurses and doctors asked more questions about my safety and depression. I continued to lie so I would be able to leave. The doctors did not examine my body because they were focused on my mental health. They did allow me to make a phone call and I dialed Anthony's number. He continued to tell me to cooperate with the doctors and to come back to him. He told me that this was a setup from my parents because they wanted me to go away to an institution.

Anthony had me believing that my parents were trying to harm me; he wanted me to not trust them. After I got off the phone with him, I made my mind up that I had to get back to him because no one else knew me as well as him. I was allowed to get dressed. At this time, I had no knowledge of the medical field and felt scared. But when I heard Anthony's voice, I felt I was safe. I was eventually released and the officer drove me back to the restaurant. As I walked through the door, I noticed everything had already been cleaned for the night. Anthony came running out to the police car and hugged me. Samantha came running out too and she cried as she hugged me.

"I knew you would come right back," he said. "Let's go out and celebrate." Later that evening, Anthony told me that it wasn't a big deal, and that my parents were just trying to control me.

It wasn't long after that Anthony moved in on Samantha. She had a problem with her car, so he offered to help get it fixed. She didn't have the money to pay upfront, so she agreed to work for him until it was paid back off. Since I was no longer talking to my family, we began to visit hers on Sundays.

One Sunday, we were all standing and talking in Samantha's mom's kitchen when I realized that her mom thought that Anthony and Samantha were dating. He had squeezed his way into their family and charmed her mother like he did mine. So, there I was, looking like Anthony's roommate, employee, and Samantha's friend, who was just along for the ride to his new girlfriend's mother's house. I could tell it wasn't the first time he was there either, because of how comfortable he was in their home. They had a conversation about cooking that was a continued conversation from the last time he spoke to her mother. Anthony had the charm turned on to her family just like he did with mine. And I realized that he was making Samantha believe that *she* was his girlfriend.

As we were leaving, Samantha got into the passenger side seat where I normally sat. *Okay*, I thought, *that's not a big deal*. I just didn't feel like fighting. I was tired. I was *always* tired.

That night I slept in my bed upstairs and Samantha slept in the spare bedroom, where Mickey usually slept. Anthony had started to sleep on the couch after Samantha moved in, which was upsetting to me. But, again, I didn't want to fight. That night, I woke up and went downstairs to get a drink of water and saw Samantha sleeping on top of Anthony on the couch, so I ran over to them.

"This is *my* boyfriend, what are you doing?" I yelled. There was an empty beer bottle on the coffee table in front of them, so I picked it up and slammed it back down, causing it to shatter onto the carpet. And they both looked up at me, like it wasn't a big deal. So, I walked over and opened the front door with such force, it hit Anthony's purple antique couch. I screamed, "Get out now!"

It was the first time I ever showed physical anger, but I could not contain it that day. But I wasn't angry with Anthony, I was furious with Samantha. *How could someone I let live in my home with do this and think it was okay?*

I threw picture frames and whatever else I could get my hands on around the room. Anthony tried grabbing me, but I pushed him away, which made him angry. It was not acceptable for me to act this way because Anthony was the only one allowed to be physically violent. The switch flipped inside of me causing this moment of rage. I couldn't hold my emotions and thoughts in my head anymore. It was an overwhelming wave of emotions that I felt as though I could not control.

After all the screaming and crying, it was morning. I had my phone and tried to call one of my friends from high school, Amanda. She answered and agreed to pick me up. Before she arrived, Anthony picked me up and threw me over his shoulder as I kicked and screamed. He would not let me down and wouldn't allow me to pack or take any of my belongings. Samantha opened the car door and he threw me in the backseat. Anthony started the car and drove away. He drove into my hometown. He wouldn't answer any of my questions. Samantha wouldn't talk, either. She was suddenly his partner in crime.

I thought he was dropping me off at my parent's house, but we drove past. He pulled into the back of Alessia's parents' restaurant and told me Alessia's mother would know what to do for me. He made me feel like I was sick and mentally disturbed and that dropping me off there would fix everything. He got out of the car to speak to her for a few minutes without me and Samantha started to cry. After a few minutes, he came back to the car and told me to get out. I got out of the car, and Anthony and Samantha drove off.

I went inside and sat with Alessia's parents and brother. We talked about what had happened, and her mom told me that Anthony was a very bad man.

"You need to stay away from him. Anthony is no good."

A friend from my high school had just passed away overseas. I went with Alessia's mom to his funeral and saw old friends from high school for the first time in a while. Later that morning, my mom came and picked me up and took me back home. As soon as I got home, I took a shower and slept. My body was so exhausted that I felt like I had the flu. Allowing my body to rest finally felt good. I slept for two days straight. I couldn't believe how physically and mentally exhausted I was.

My parents took my phone so I wouldn't be able to contact Anthony so I logged into the computer on AOL instant messenger. Samantha had messaged me saying she and Anthony missed me and wanted me to come home. She apologized for what had happened, and I decided that Anthony needed me. In my mind, I had to get back to him right away. I didn't know it, but I was brainwashed. Anything Anthony wanted me to do or think, I did. Looking back today, I realize that Anthony deliberately made me feel disoriented, dependent, and worthless. It was as if he programmed me to be this way. Anthony took over my mind by blocking me from making decisions, keeping me overworked and tired and, in my case, malnourished. Anthony would continue to call me "stupid," and I believed I was. Brainwashing made it nearly impossible to leave, because Anthony made me believe I was crazy and "needed" him for comfort. But in reality, he was source of my suffering. During this separation, I felt lost and empty because he became my person, and he was suddenly "gone."

Anthony messaged and told me to leave my parent's house right, that they would pick me up at the bottom of the hill. I got dressed, put my shoes on, and started walking out after telling my mom that I was leaving. My parents and their friends, who were visiting, tried talking me into staying. At this point, they all saw what Anthony had done to me. They all saw the control. But because I was a legal adult, they couldn't force me to stay. I started walking down the hill and knocked on the door of a trailer by the creek. A man answered the door and I asked if I could use his phone. He was friendly, agreed, and let me wait there for them to pick me up. I got a hold of Anthony and he was there to pick me up within thirty minutes. I was back in the truck with Anthony again, and it was just the two of us.

"Things are going to be different now," he said. "I want you to think of me as a father figure and not a boyfriend."

I listened. I *always* listened.

"No one will be sleeping in *my* bed except me," he said. "From now on, you will sleep in the spare bedroom and Samantha will sleep on the couch."

He was in complete control. And he knew it.

··· Chapter Four

One night, I was deep asleep on a tan suede flimsy worn out futon in the spare room. It was pitch dark in the room and I woke up to the door creaking open slowly. Anthony immediately said, "shhhhhh." I had no clue what to expect because he strictly told me how he wanted me to view him as a father figure. But here he was, undressing me. Anthony was always in charge and only he could change the roles and rules of his game. It was becoming emotionally exhausting trying to keep up with these games. But I wanted to please so I kissed him back. I assumed it meant we were back together again. I felt happy but feared abandonment and not being good enough for him. We had sex but he told me not to tell anyone—it was our secret. Later that day, at the restaurant, I was talking to Samantha, and she asked how I was doing being back at the house.

"Anthony and I slept together last night!" I was so excited that I blurted it out. She looked deep into my eyes.

"What the hell!" she yelled and stormed out of the restaurant. Anthony came back and asked what had happened. I told him what I told her. He was angry that I didn't keep our secret. Anthony talked Samantha into coming back to work that evening and she seemed happier. He was sly and charming, and so smooth that he could make anyone believe they were the only one who mattered to him. He was in an exceptionally good mood that night at the restaurant and let us drink as we worked. When everything was cleaned up after we closed, he made more drinks. Everyone left, except the three of us.

We continued to drink until he told us to go next door for a few more drinks before we met him back at the house. Once we were all home, Anthony got out his pack of cards and wanted to play a game. It was his version of War, but if you got the lower card you had to strip or take a shot. Samantha and I were both very intoxicated at that point. But he was in such a good mood that I didn't want him to become angry, so I continued to do as he asked. Eventually, he dared Samantha and I to kiss. We both had to strip down to nothing first. He then took us upstairs and had sex with both of us.

One afternoon, I brought Mickey back to the house once we closed the restaurant after the lunch crowd left, to rest before we had to go return to reopen for dinner. I went to tidy up and make the bed and found a pair of women's underwear on the floor that weren't mine. They had to be Samantha's. Something inside of me clicked, and I wanted Samantha out. I grabbed a few trash bags, filled them with her belongings, put them out on the front porch. When she arrived back to the house, I told her I wanted her gone and she seemed like she wanted to go too. Anthony was constantly yelling at her for smoking cigarettes. She didn't want to work for him anymore because he had stopped paying her too. So, she took all her belongings and left. Our friendship ended that day. I never expected it to happen, especially with someone I went to school with. We were just young naïve girls, but in my mind, it was never Anthony's fault for cheating. It was always the girl he cheated with.

I had two other friends that I had graduated high school with who needed jobs, and also began working for Anthony. My friend Amanda worked one night but he refused pay her. Instead, he got her and me drunk and tried to play his card game. But Amanda was a close friend and I made sure that didn't happen. It was the one time that I didn't care if Anthony was mad, because what he was doing was wrong. She tried to stay in contact, because she saw the kind of person Anthony was, begging me to leave him. But I didn't listen.

My childhood friend Jess worked for him another night. After we closed the restaurant, Anthony told me to go home, saying he would come soon after. I listened to him. He came home late and woke me up to say Jess was a bad friend, and that I shouldn't talk to her anymore. Years later I discovered that he'd taken her to a strip club and bar, slipped something in her drink, and tried to kiss her. She called her boyfriend, and he arrived with her mom before she was so sedated. She later shared that he didn't allow her to take her phone into the club or bar.

It quickly became a pattern that my friends vanished; they didn't want to be around Anthony. I saw how he hurt them and knew my family was hurting, but I still could not leave him. I truly believed I was the only one who could heal him and his anger. I could "fix" him. I believed he *could* change. People *do* change. *Right?*

One day, Anthony and I went for a day trip up to New York to visit his father. We stopped at his father's house in a neighborhood called South Jamaica in Queens. I felt uncomfortable walking up the dirty street to his row home. We walked through two sets of large doors to get into his house. The inside was dark, outdated, and dusty; not at all what I had imagined. We walked over old wooden creaky floors with dust balls tumbling across them. The house was cramped with old paintings and smelled funny. Upon seeing him, he looked like an older version of Anthony, with thick coke bottle glasses, a button-up dress shirt, suspenders, worn-out brown leather shoes, with a head full of white hair and a big white beard. Anthony had said he used to be a big-time artist.

Throughout the visit, he kept telling me how pretty I was and ordered his wife to bring us drinks. We sat and talked in his living room that was filled with oversized antique tables and Victorian couches placed on large dirty area rugs. The windows were covered with dark green curtains that kept light from coming in. Anthony seemed noticeably uncomfortable, so we eventually walked to a pizza shop down the street for lunch.

After we left, we stopped at Anthony's friend's house in Long Island. Joey and Anthony had been friends since grade school. I met Joey, his wife Yvette, and their kids. As I was sitting and talking to Yvette, she asked if Anthony had gotten to see his son yet. *What?* Anthony has a *son?* To my surprise Anthony had *two* kids. I knew he never married Mickey's mother, and I later found out that his son was three years old at the time. When I asked Anthony about his son, he told me that he had gotten divorced about a year ago. He had never mentioned he was previously married.

"My wife cheated on me with a painter when we were renovating our new home in New Jersey." He became sidetracked and started talking about how his home in New Jersey sat off the golf course and the next-door neighbors were state senators. He continued to tell me how her family destroyed him, and they were the reason he couldn't see his son without court supervision. The story was truly sad and heartbreaking, his eyes even welled up with tears for a moment. Then he suddenly slapped me in the face and told me to never ask about his son or ex-wife again. We later drove back home in silence.

On his thirty-first birthday, Anthony wanted to take his boat out on the river. When we first met, he lied to me about his age and told me he was twenty-nine. I saw later his license laying on the counter and did the math myself. I asked him why he lied about his age, and he played it off like it was no big deal.

"It sounded better to say I was twenty-nine since you were eighteen." He proceeded to say that age was just a number before muttering, "I told my ex-wife I would find someone much younger, like an 18-year-old."

He wanted to invite only Vicki and me for his birthday celebration. She came to the house and we had a mini birthday cake that she brought, along with a card. She still believed I was Anthony's roommate and seemed as though she were still pursuing him. I didn't want him to be upset on his birthday weekend, so I went with what he told me to do. We picked up alcohol at the store on the way to the boat, and brought Ferelli with us.

Anthony backed the boat into the water and parked the truck while Vicki and I tied the boat up to the dock. Anthony jumped onto the boat, and we took off down the river. He found a spot, put the anchor down, and shut the engine off. We turned on music, laid in the sun, cooked on the grill, and went swimming with Ferelli in a small area by the riverside.

Towards the evening, we packed everything up, loaded the boat on the trailer, and drove back home. After drinking all day in the sun, we were tired but Anthony wanted to keep the party going. He got some alcohol out and Vicki and I started throwing back shots. She started kissing me. I wanted to keep Anthony happy, and before I knew it the three of us were upstairs.

Afterwards, I got up and took a shower. I felt depressed and disgusted. I didn't want to live that way anymore. I turned the water on as hot as I could handle it, before collapsing to the floor of the bathtub to cry. I pulled my knees up into my chest and hugged myself, with my head down until the water turned cold. I didn't care what was going on in the bedroom, I knew he was having sex with her again. And it made me feel used and numb. No one came to check on me to see if I was okay. Eventually, I got up, dried off and got dressed. I went downstairs to find Anthony asleep on one couch and Vicki asleep on the other.

The following morning, she was gone, and I told Anthony that I didn't want to keep having threesomes. He told me that I was good at it and his ex-wife used to do it too. He wanted me to think that doing this was a normal part of life. He told me that Vicki liked girls and wasn't interested in him. I now believe he had conditioned Vicki to like girls and was trying to condition me too, even though I didn't see it back then. It continued to happen, more times than I would like to admit. And each time, I felt more and more numb. It became another chore to keep Anthony happy; I feared him when he was angry.

The verbal and physical abuse became more intense and frequent. The verbal abuse was daily. He called me stupid, and I started to believe perhaps something *was* wrong with me. Anthony told me I was getting too skinny and looked ugly. He said my body looked like a boy's, without any curves. He controlled what I ate and how much I ate. I always had to carry my phone, and if I didn't answer, he got very agitated. Anthony started screaming at me in the restaurant one afternoon.

"What the hell is wrong with you? You are so fucking stupid! Something is wrong with you! Do you understand English? Can you hear me?"

He slapped the side of my head and ended the conversation. My ears rang and I began having trouble hearing. When he continued to yell, my ears started to ring more. I became dizzy and felt like I was going to pass out. I thought that maybe I was losing my hearing and should get that looked at by a doctor. Maybe something *was* wrong with me, and I needed to fix it. If that *was* the problem, and if I fixed it, Anthony couldn't be mad anymore. I made an appointment with an ear, nose, and throat doctor that week. They did tests for hearing and ordered an MRI scan. I drove myself to get the MRI of my brain done in the morning. They started an intravenous line and ran contrast dye through my veins during the scan, and I had a reaction and instantly felt sick and dizzy. I was too afraid to call and bother Anthony to come pick me up since he was busy working. I decided that I was okay to drive myself home.

I later called Anthony and told him that I was sick and couldn't go to work. He became outraged and started screaming on the phone, calling me names. I was trying to sleep upstairs but kept feeling nauseated after the MRI. At one point, I woke up when the front door opened and I heard a woman's voice. It was Vicki's. Within minutes I could hear them having sex downstairs. Moments later, Vicki came up the stairs and went into the bathroom. When she came out, she saw me but didn't say a word, she was also under Anthony's control. She continued down the stairs and they both left.

I began to dread the weekends because it meant time alone with Ferelli in the house. I wasn't physically locked inside the house but my access to my phone or a car was taken away from me most of the time. I still didn't have my own car so I couldn't come and go as I wanted. Anthony stopped coming home on Friday and Saturday nights. He often told me he was going to Betty's house to help her. Anthony had left his camera at the house one weekend, and I was looking at pictures on it. I came across naked pictures of Vicki on a white sheep skin rug in our house. He was taking these pictures when he would keep me at the restaurant by myself during the lunch breaks while he had his afternoon fun with Vicki. The pictures had the dates and times on them. Finding these made me sick but when confronted, Anthony had an excuse. He lightly said they were pictures she wanted for a modeling profile and continued with whatever he was doing.

In my mind, at that time, all I cared about was that I was with Anthony. Today, I understand that trauma bonding is the formation of an emotional attachment between a person and their abuser. My attachment pattern with Anthony at the time alternated between devaluation and intimacy. He was the person I wanted to console me the most while he was also hurting me the greatest. In trauma bonding it looks like a compulsive cycle of wanting to please your partner, and I pleased Anthony by doing whatever he wanted me to do to avoid setting him off. I was tricked by Anthony's sweet and caring phase in the beginning, which made me believe that I would be loved and protected by him.

We used to bring Ferelli with us to the restaurant and he slept by the door in the kitchen. He was growing and getting bigger and when he laid by the door, sometimes you could hear the door move from out in the dining area.

"If Ferelli keeps making noises with the door you better just get out of my face and leave the restaurant right now!" Anthony yelled one day.

He took out all his anger on me for something I had no control over. I was starting to get annoyed, and I yelled back at him that there was no way I could control Ferelli when I was trying to work. Anthony grabbed me by the arm and told me that I was stupid and to fix the problem now. I became so frustrated that I just bolted out the back door of the kitchen and kept running. I ran in my high heels down the alleys and to the cement stairs that led down to the river where there was another walking path. I kept on running up North Front Street by the river until the walkway ended. I stopped for a minute to catch my breath and thought Anthony would come looking for me, but he never did. I decided to keep running and when I reached the street, I kept walking fast. It was starting to get dark out and a few cars honked their horns or stopped and asked if I wanted a ride. I declined. I did not have a phone with me because I left it laying on the bar in the restaurant. The street that I continued to walk up was a busy street that connected to highways. With it being dark out and I was wearing all black I'm surprised today that I didn't get hit by a car because I had to cross a few times. Anthony never came looking. I had no idea how many hours had passed. It was almost eight miles from the restaurant to our house. Today I ask myself, "Why did I run to our house and not fully away from Anthony?" I guess I never felt or knew that I had that option. I made it home and sat on the front porch steps and cried with my head down in my lap. I sat for what seemed like a few more hours. I heard the loud sound of his truck in the distance. Anthony drove up the driveway. He got out of the truck and walked over.

"Are you done?" he asked in a calm voice.

I nodded and went inside for a shower. Once inside he looked at me and started to scream and yell about how he needed help at the restaurant. I let him scream at me and went upstairs to sleep. Many more instances like this continued to happen. I got upset with him yelling at me and I walked out the front door and started walking down the street. I had no idea where I was going but I felt like I had to walk away from him. I didn't have a car but I had legs. Anthony got in his truck and told me, "Stop what you're doing. You look ridiculous. Just get in the truck." I refused at first but always eventually got into his truck. He made it known that I had no one. I had him and only he knew the real me.

"Your parents and friends will never understand you the way I do," he would say. "I cured your depression and if you stayed with your parents and friends, you would just be a loser with no life."

For some reason I knew I had to walk away from him, but I was so weak, and he pulled me back to him with all the right persuasive words. I soon began to fear that if I didn't do what Anthony wanted that he would become mad and physically or mentally abusive to me. I knew that I had to avoid that at all costs. I had to be the perfect girlfriend for him. Vicki started to get the idea that I was with Anthony, and she backed off and began to date other people but still helped Anthony in the restaurant. Without knowing it, I had become Anthony's slave. I cleaned the entire house, washed all the cars, mowed the lawn, and ran his restaurant. I was so tired that I had no time to think of what was really happening. I never had the time to process that I was in a domestic violence relationship. Not due to the physical exhaustion, but also the toxic dynamics and constant manipulation that drained me mentally.

Every day at the restaurant Anthony became more and more paranoid. He sat at a table outside and told me that the people walking by were FBI agents and that they were watching his every move. He thought that they were taking pictures of us. If men in suits walked by the restaurant slowly, he automatically thought that they were FBI or undercover police officers by the shoes they wore. He told me that FBI guys do not wear rubber sole shoes. I always thought that was strange. I knew that Anthony did not have a good relationship with the lady that he leased his restaurant building from. They yelled back and forth at each other frequently. He never paid the rent on time, and she eventually took him to court.

That November, Anthony was ordered to vacate the building within ten days. He lost his restaurant; he lost his empire. The last week it was open, he was barely there. So, I ran the restaurant myself to earn as much as possible during those last days. Anthony had more than enough money to pay his monthly lease, but only chose to pay when he wanted.

It was a very cold evening when we packed everything up and put it into storage. Vicki, Anthony's brother, Betty, and I packed it all up in one night. It was unbelievable that we packed an entire restaurant up in such a short time; we were there until after midnight. The questions going through my mind that evening was, "What was going to happen next? How were we going to make money now? How were we going to pay for the rent on our house?" The restaurant made a lot of money, but Anthony never saved any of it. Instead, he spent it on expensive and lavish items for himself.

Anthony told me that I had to think about what I wanted to do in my life, and I felt like he was getting rid of me. He told me to call Amanda and go live with her, so I called and she welcomed me with open arms. She expressed how much she hated Anthony; she said he was an awful person who talked badly about me to her when she worked for him. She had so much anger towards him. I then called my parents and told them I was going to move in with Amanda and I wanted to go back to school. They agreed to help me, if I agreed to stay away from Anthony. I moved in with Amanda later that month. She helped me get a job and life began to look up. But ... I just couldn't stay away from Anthony. Every day, he stopped at the hotel I worked at to help himself to coffee and breakfast, and cash out of my wallet, saying he needed it for gas.

"I can't see you anymore or my parents will not help me get back on my feet," I told him one day.

Even though I knew I was supposed to stay away from him, I just couldn't. He made me feel loved again. The physical abuse had stopped, and we were back in a "reconciliation phase." Even though he had sent me away, I was still under his control. I remembered our good times and often fantasized about our day trips to the beach or New York City when we laughed and held hands. I began to tell myself that the bad times weren't "that bad." Luckily, I was very fortunate to have people in my life who fought for me, even when I wasn't able.

My favorite person in our family was my grandpa "Pappy." He was the one who taught me how to shoot a gun, garden, work hard, and the importance of what an education can do for you. My grandpa was retired from being the Director of Education for a youth development center for juvenile delinquent males who were court-ordered to serve time. The center where he worked served a population of more aggressive youth, typically with antisocial values who need an increased level of security. They provided education to students ages twelve to twenty-one who were expected to continue their education as part of the treatment program. This allowed students to return to the community with an enhanced self-image and functioning as a socially productive member in society. By doing this job, he was able to see who Anthony really was when he first met him. Anthony had admitted to me that he had served time in a juvenile detention center during his teens.

Every time Anthony had tried to separate me from my family, my grandpa was there. I did try to leave Anthony and was staying at my parents' house. One day, he drove up my parents' driveway in his old black antique forties Chevy pickup truck with Mickey in the passenger seat and yelled for me to get in. This was one of the times where I tried to get away from Anthony. My parents and grandpa were in the driveway yelling for me to stay, while Anthony was demanding me to get in the truck. Mickey was only eleven years old at the time and should not have had to witness that. I didn't know what to do, so I got in. Anthony put the truck in reverse and spun the tires down the driveway kicking up dirt and gravel.

My grandpa was later diagnosed with lung cancer and declined quickly. I believe that if he knew he didn't have a lot of time left he may have tried to save me that day. I thank God that I was able to see him before he passed. My grandpa taught me to never give up on my goals, keep my chin up, and never stop moving. And that is exactly what I did.

Soon I saved up enough money to get my own apartment. It was a starter apartment; a ground floor unit with one bedroom. The rent was cheap, but it was my own place. My parents gave me a car to use and helped me move in, and I enrolled back at the local community college to further my path in nursing. Balancing a full-time semester with a full-time job was often challenging, but I was happy and felt *almost* independent again.

Once I finished the semester, I applied to get into nursing school clinicals. I was at work the day I received a phone call for my acceptance to start that fall. It was such great news! I called my mom to share the news before calling Anthony, and he was upset that I didn't call him first and began to yell at me. My happiness suddenly became all about him. He didn't offer to celebrate with me, instead he attempted to take away my excitement. That day, I was proud and happy about my accomplishment, and couldn't understand why he wasn't too. But a narcissist is a thief of joy, and today I understand that Anthony's biggest fear was that my happiness wasn't always about him. He desperately needed to be the center of attention ... and if he wasn't, it meant that he didn't have complete control over me.

One weekend when I had time off, Anthony and I drove by an old house near a creek in Hershey with a "for sale by owner" sign in the front yard. It was a large brick home but required significant renovation. Anthony had already negotiated a sales agreement with the owner, having borrowed money from an undisclosed source. He refused to tell me where the money came from and insisted that it be put in my name, but I was too excited to care too much because we had just bought our first house!

At the time my parents didn't know that I was seeing Anthony, I was pretending that our relationship was over. Since my nursing clinicals were an hour away, I stayed with my sister during the weekdays. And during the weekends, I stayed at our new house in Hershey and lied to my parents saying that I was staying with Amanda.

Before moving in, Mickey and I packed up the house that Anthony and I had rented together, and loaded everything into the back of a big pickup truck. We had to make multiple trips back and forth from Harrisburg to Hershey. Anthony showed up to help put the couches on the trailer and was gone again. Every weekend, I helped Anthony with renovations. The house was filled with black mold, so I scrubbed the walls with bleach (which I later developed breathing issues from). It felt like for the first time we were working together as a couple; as a team. I had my own purpose in life again and he had his own projects. I met his business partner Martin. Together, they had bought another restaurant in hopes of turning it into something like his old one.

One day, we visited with Martin at his house and met his family. He looked to be in his fifties and introduced us to his new Ukrainian bride … who looked to be eighteen. She was a petite young blonde girl that appeared to be very timid. I could tell right away, there was something not quite right with him. Martin talked fast and seemed to have high bursts of energy as he spoke, as though he were on cocaine or unprescribed Adderall. He was short with dyed jet black dyed hair that looked like it came from a box of "just for men" box. I learned later that he was the undisclosed source that fronted the money to buy our house, as well as the building they were renovating into the new restaurant, which needed as much work done as our house. Fortunately, the building already obtained a liquor license.

I eventually told my parents that I was back with Anthony. They were devastated but knew it this was my choice. I'm sure they may have already suspected it because I was barely talking to them again. I told them Anthony had changed, and that we had good things happening. I loved school and was making new friends, however, I didn't realize I was beginning to hold people at a distance again. They often asked me to join them after clinicals, to go eat or study. But I always turned them down because I was sure if Anthony wouldn't approve of me hanging out with people he had never met before.

I was halfway through nursing school and on break for the summer when Anthony decided that he wanted to buy a new pickup truck to help with all the renovations. We drove to Lancaster to work out a deal at a Dodge dealership. Anthony was the kind of person to try to squeeze every penny out of a salesman, so he went back and forth negotiating with him for hours. Eventually, we left without a truck. The next morning, Anthony told me to get dressed because we are going to get married. My mouth dropped to the floor. I had dreamed about us getting married and began to ask questions.

"Don't you want a wedding?"

"Aren't you supposed to propose to me?"

He told me it was going to happen anyway, and that I should just get dressed ... so I did.

We drove to a small courthouse to meet one of his friends, who was a judge. We were called into the courtroom, where a teenager pled guilty to something, with his parents beside him. They quickly became guests to our very small wedding. When the judge said, "You may kiss your bride," Anthony gave me a small peck on the lips. It seemed he was rushing to get the paperwork and get us out of there as soon as possible. It was surreal. There was no beautiful white dress, we were wearing everyday clothes. Afterwards, we went to eat at a local restaurant, but without friends and family to celebrate with. It happened so fast, it felt like a dream. But not the dream I had envisioned.

The next day after we woke up, Anthony told me to get dressed to go back to the Dodge dealership. He quickly showed our marriage license to the same salesman he was negotiating with a few days before, and he agreed to offer an additional discount on the truck. At the time, I couldn't process what had just happened. After leaving, Anthony promised that we would soon celebrate with our families.

"We will have a huge party," he said. "I know that you are the one for me." He continued on to share how he married his ex in Vegas and had a big reception afterwards with family and friends. *Why would I want to hear about that?*

After we were married, everything had to be in my name. Utilities. Vehicles. Insurance. Everything. He told me nothing could ever be in his name. At the time, I thought he had bad credit due to a bankruptcy or something. He explained that we needed to build my credit, so we could live more comfortably.

That summer went by quickly. I interned at Hershey Medical Center on a medical surgical floor; it was my foot in the door for my future job as a registered nurse. The nurses I worked with were wonderful, it was a positive learning experience. Anthony and I had the first floor of the house nearly finished. We opened the floor plan and put in hardwood floors, a beautiful tile floor in the bathroom and an elegant raised bowel sink. The kitchen had granite counters and all new stainless-steel appliances. I decorated and it felt like home. I thought it odd that Anthony didn't want any photos of us displayed, but decided not to ask why.

That fall I stayed at Anthony's mom's house during the week to continue my nursing clinicals and stayed in one of the spare bedrooms. She worked during the day, while I was in school. But when I was at the house, I made sure to tidy up after myself and mostly stayed in the bedroom to study. I went to sleep early so I could wake early and return to the hospital. We often talked in the evenings, and she asked me medical questions. She was excited that Anthony and I were married and didn't seem to think it was strange that we married in a courtroom on a whim. She continued to gossip and tell me about Anthony's ex-wife and girlfriends. He was always the victim in her stories, she believed he never did any wrong.

One weekday I decided to spend the night at our house and drove home. I had a very important exam the following afternoon, which meant I could sleep in. I woke and showered the next morning before going downstairs for breakfast. I asked Anthony how the restaurant was coming along. If I asked the wrong question, or if he was having a stressful day, it led to him becoming infuriated. Today, I understand these moments are defined as the "tension building phase" of the cycle of abuse. Asking too many questions at once triggered him, often moving us into the "incident of abuse phase." After this it quickly turned into the incident of abuse phase.

That morning, he ran at me full force. Terrified, I turned and ran toward the staircase. The stairs were wooden, which made me slip in socks, and he pinned me down. He grabbed my hair and slammed the side of my head into the wall. I didn't know he was holding a pair of scissors in his other hand. He grabbed a large handful of my hair and cut it off. His eyes were smiling as I screamed, and he let me go. I ran up to the bathroom and cried. My chest felt tight and I tried to breathe, for a moment I felt frozen in time. Soon after, Anthony left the house as if nothing happened. I threw my hair back into a ponytail, pulled myself together physically and mentally, and drove to school to take my exam ... also like nothing happened.

My last two semesters of school flew by, even though nursing school was tough and often stressful. The instructors were intimidating, but they didn't phase me because I was going through deeper intimidation at home. One that no one knew about. I graduated the following summer and landed my first nursing job at Hershey Medical Center. My family came for my graduation, but after the ceremony we didn't go out to celebrate. Anthony said he had to get back to the restaurant, and since he couldn't go, he didn't want me to either.

I started working on the medical surgical floor where I completed my internship and took care of patients needing transplants, as well as cardiac, surgical oncology and colorectal procedures. A few weeks later, I took my nursing boards test and passed. Anthony continued to have no words of encouragement, or even so much as a kind word to wish me luck beforehand. Narcissists maintain an unrealistic self-image and that causes them to believe their intelligence is superior to others. Anthony often bragged about his "high IQ," saying I possessed an average level of intelligence, so he did not view my passing my boards as a significant accomplishment.

Through all the dark times, Anthony and I did manage to share some wonderful memories too. For my twenty-third birthday, he planned a surprise party, but he only invited his family. He cooked and bought presents. We laughed, ate, and went to bed happy in each other's arms. It made me believe that he really was trying to change. It seemed those few years were good between us. We only fought less and made up quickly. Despite having to constantly report my whereabouts, and having no control over how my paychecks were spent and the lack of money left over, I still *thought* I was happy.

Anthony worked late nights but came home every night. Until one night in the fall, he didn't. He wasn't picking up his phone, as I tried again and again. It wasn't like him. I tried calling till well after midnight. Still, no answer. He finally came home late the next day, saying he had too much to drink at a friend's house and his phone died. But my gut told me something wasn't right, so I continued to ask questions. He grabbed my hair and slammed my head so hard into the wall—so hard it left an indent in the drywall—and continued until his hands began hurting and I saw stars and black dots. Injuries to the head remain hidden to the public eye, making them ideal for an abuser.

Once he stopped, I ran upstairs and cried. Chunks of hair covered the back of my shirt. After I took my clothes off and stepped into a hot shower, more chunks washed down the drain. I could already feel the fresh sores and bumps on my head. I got dressed and went to sleep. Later, Anthony came upstairs and apologized, saying he was sorry and kissing my head. That night, we quickly moved full circle, from the "calm phase" all the way through to the "reconciliation phase" and back again.

That winter, Anthony's leg that was injured in his "secret" accident began to cause him pain, the area where the screws were in his ankle had become swollen and inflamed due to hours of working on his feet. I called and made an appointment for him to have it looked at, and surgery was quickly scheduled to take out the hardware and screws. Anthony was told not to eat or drink anything past midnight before the surgery. He didn't listen and ended up aspirating food while under anesthesia, causing him to have to spend the night in the hospital instead of being discharged the same day as scheduled. I stayed with him overnight, sleeping in the uncomfortable chair next to his bedside. I felt that I had to make sure he was alright and that he had everything he needed.

We went home the next day and Anthony refused to rest. His friend Bob came to the house, wanting one of his trailers back that Anthony had borrowed to move a large stone fountain. The fountain was still on the trailer and they needed to use a skid loader to remove it from the trailer. Anthony did not want him to touch the fountain pieces in fear that they would break. Bob became frustrated with Anthony because he wanted his trailer back, he needed it for a project. I was upstairs cleaning the bathroom when I heard them screaming at each other downstairs. I became worried and started to walk down the stairs and into the kitchen.

"Did you tell Rebecca about where you were the other night?" Bob yelled at Anthony when he saw me. "Did you tell her about the girl you have been fucking?"

Anthony slammed the door in Bob's face and locked it.

"What is Bob talking about?" I asked.

Anthony made up a story, saying Bob was just jealous of him. Seeing that I wasn't believing him, he began scream at me. But since he was in so much pain from surgery, he couldn't run after and hurt me. I put the pieces together in my head that Anthony most likely cheated on me that night that he didn't answer my calls or come home. After that day, the abuse was worse than ever. Every little inconvenience set Anthony off, and I was slapped, pushed, or kicked. Anthony healed quickly from surgery and was back to his projects of fixing the house and restaurant.

When Anthony had the old restaurant, he had bought a horse for Mickey that she named Dakota. Anthony found a small farm owned by an elderly couple about a mile down the road from our house. The farm didn't have any animals, but the pasture was fenced in. He made a deal with the owner to let us keep Dakota there for a monthly fee. In time, Anthony had talked this older couple into selling their farm to him. Anthony wrote up a very long detailed contract and soon took over the mortgage payments. The older couple moved off the farm and it became ours.

We kept the horse at the farm, which involved more work. Anthony decided that he wanted to renovate the entire farmhouse and had three major projects going at that time. He didn't like to hire independent contractors to help him, so the projects were always on hold. When Anthony did hire someone, the work was never done the way he wanted so he refused to pay them, which happened frequently. And, unfortunately, they lost less money by walking away than by taking Anthony to court. Narcissists are perfectionists that demand flawless performances. There wasn't a single contractor that was able to complete their job without Anthony complaining or critiquing them.

One weekend, he wanted to travel to Ohio to buy a wolf hybrid puppy. He said he needed this type of breed to protect the property, so we drove hours away to a special breeder. When we arrived, there were several wolf hybrid dogs and puppies, and they were beautiful. Some were mixed Huskies, and others were mixed German Shepherds. There was even one that sat tall and majestic; it looked just like a wolf. Anthony began to negotiate with the breeder, so he wouldn't have to pay full asking price for an eight-week-old puppy. She agreed to show us some mixed German Shepherd puppies that were around three months old, and Anthony told me to pick one out. It was rare that he allowed me to make choices, so I reveled in it for a moment. The puppy I picked was very eight-six percent wolf, so I named him Wolf. He was very shy and hid under the seat in the back of the car during the whole drive back home.

Wolf was difficult to train and tested Anthony by growling at him. Eventually, Anthony began to hit him when he growled. When I was home, I spent as much time with him as possible because I was afraid he'd become aggressive without love and affection. Anthony kept Wolf chained to a tree with a very heavy thick chain around his neck. The way Anthony treated our dogs bothered me deeply, so I gave them extra treats when he wasn't around. It wasn't until later that I discovered Anthony had past charges of animal cruelty.

One afternoon Anthony and I were outside on the back porch, joking and talking. I was playing with the dogs on the deck when Anthony thought it would be funny to point his BB gun, that looked like a real handgun, at my head. In fear, I asked him to point it away from me, and pushed his arm away. The dogs had begun to sense when Anthony was angry, so they ran off into the yard. I didn't know it then, but we were back in the "tension building phase" in the cycle of abuse. The deck was six feet high up from the ground and didn't have a railing or stairs yet, so the edge was a drop off.

Anthony didn't like that I pushed his arm away, so he pushed me off the deck, and we quickly moved into the "incident of violence phase." I landed on my knees and hands in the grass, the wind was knocked out of me. As I sat there, Anthony shot me. He continued to shoot me multiple times in the back of the head, one BB after another, until he stopped to refill his gun. I couldn't scream, I was stunned by what was happening. And I tried to get onto my feet, but was sore from the fall and couldn't, so I crawled towards the road to get help. Anthony continued to shoot at me, aiming for my head. When he finally stopped, I had bumps all over my head, back, and neck. My head was sore with welts, I saw stars and became nauseated. I heard him start his diesel truck and drive off. I rolled onto my back in the grass and closed my eyes, listening to my quick breath.

In the silence, the birds chirped in the distance near the creek. My dogs ran over and licked my face. I slowly rose to my feet, brushed off the dirt and grass, and made my way straight to the shower to cry. As I shampooed my hair, my entire head was covered in welts. It hurt to comb my hair, so I left it tangled, got dressed, and fell into my bed in pain. We usually moved quickly into the "reconciliation phase," but instead of apologizing, he drove away.

I continued to tell myself that it would be okay, despite the weekly beatings I endured. It was impossible to accept my reality, so I lived in denial and shrugged it off.

"I'm sorry, it doesn't have to be this way if you would just listen to me," he would say.

When Anthony told me he wanted a family, it gave me hope that he would change.

Maybe having a baby would bring us closer.

··· Chapter Five

One September, I found out I was pregnant. My friends at work kept telling me that I had all the signs and symptoms of pregnancy, including nausea and major fatigue. My clinical head nurse went out and bought a pregnancy test and told me to go take it right away. I did and yes, I was *finally* pregnant. It had taken almost a full year.

I was ecstatic and called Anthony right away.

"Oh, good," he said flatly.

After I arrived back home after work, I ran up to him in the driveway and hugged him, crying with joy. But he was cold and distant. I asked if we could go out to dinner to celebrate, and he angrily said that he didn't have the time or money. Then he turned to me and punched me hard in the stomach. I fell to the ground; the wind knocked out of me, it felt like I had stopped breathing. Still laying on the ground, I froze and couldn't move. I started to cry and he walked away. He got in his truck and drove away. If we were ever to have a happy moment and celebrate together, it should have been then … the day we learned that we were going to bring a new life into the world. But that dream was crushed. *I* felt crushed. And I was scared to tell my family.

The next morning, I offered to help Anthony install the trim and tile in the kitchen. If I didn't hold a piece of wood up correctly, he lost his temper and began yelling that I was stupid and the one reason I was a nurse was because he let me become one.

In my profession, we regularly learn new things and asking questions can be a necessity. But whenever I asked Anthony questions, he became angry. He would pick up whatever was around him, no matter it's value or sentiment, and break it. He threw objects across the room, and they broke or shattered everywhere. One day, Anthony became so angry he slammed the front door so hard that he broke the glass out of the square panes. It shattered to pieces everywhere inside and outside the house, and I had to clean it up. I was always cleaning up his messes.

After working a long night shift, I walked into our house around eight in the morning, and Ferelli was not waiting by the door for me as he always was. There was an eerie silence in the house, so I walked over to Ferelli's bed and called for him to get up, but he didn't move. I walked closer and saw that he wasn't breathing. I yelled up the stairs to Anthony, he came running down, and I started to cry. My best friend was gone. Without any emotion, Anthony took him outside and buried him. The house was quiet without him and I cried for weeks. After a while, Anthony came home with another puppy ... a Doberman that I named Pinch. That's when I realized, everything and everyone was replaceable in Anthony's world.

Later that month, our neighborhood received major flood warnings. We had a creek in our backyard, so we anticipated that our house would likely flood as it did before we began renovations. The night before the storm, we brought in everything we could, from the decorative garden lights to the farm equipment in the backyard. We cleared everything off the porches and moved our valuables upstairs. That evening, the water rapidly rose up to the back deck, and our backyard disappeared. We stayed up all night with the generator on and I called off work.

Early the next morning, Anthony moved the vehicles and boats out of the garage and over to our farm down the road where they would be safe. Only hours later, I noticed the water was coming inside the house, so I ran outside to tell Anthony to turn the electricity off. The next thing I knew, water rushed in and our furniture was floating. Anthony told me to pack a bag as he grabbed our important papers from the safe. By the time I came back downstairs, the water was up to my waist. I grabbed Pinch, put him on a leash, and pushed through the cold dirty moving current to get to the road. Anthony went back inside the house to move his gold leaf Victorian couch upstairs with the help of a friend. Anthony and his friend made it back out just before the first level of the house was completely under water. Wolf was still upstairs in the bedroom.

That evening, Anthony returned with a small boat and a jet ski to rescue him. Shortly after, the floodwaters reached the second-story ceiling, inundating the entire house. Anthony's restaurant, located near the river, was also submerged. Fortunately, he had flood insurance for both properties. He quickly filed claimed to collect on the properties as soon as possible. It seemed all he ever cared about was money and his possessions.

Our horse trailer had a camper with a kitchen, bedroom, and full shower. Anthony informed me that he would live in the camper while he worked on repairing the restaurant and the house, making it clear that he didn't want me staying with him. He insisted that I stay with my parents instead. I had recently told them about my pregnancy, and they were happy for me. At least that was what they said.

I took two weeks off work and drove to the flooded house every morning to check on Anthony, bringing him food and coffee. The neighborhood pulled together during that time. Every evening the restaurants took turns catering meals for the entire town; everyone worked together to help everyone out. Some members of a local church even volunteered to help Anthony gut our entire house. They worked all day and night, and in return Anthony gave them nothing.

While Anthony cleaned the restaurant, he spent his time with a young pretty blonde named Natasha who looked about eighteen. She was from Ukraine and spoke little English—or so she said. She had a muscular build and wore bright blue eyeshadow and red lipstick. I didn't know how Anthony met her, but suspected he was being unfaithful again. I spent much of my pregnancy feeling sick and exhausted, so I was too tired and afraid to confront him about it.

While staying at my parent's house, I stayed in the basement, which had been converted into a small apartment. Anthony asked me to get on the computer to make an itemized list of everything we had in the house, along with its value, for the insurance company. After signing into his personal email, I saw emails in his inbox from someone named Lana saying how much fun she had with him that summer. She wrote about how they "made love" at his restaurant and how much she missed him. My stomach dropped and I ran to the bathroom to vomit. Looking back, I should have saved the emails and divorced Anthony. Instead, I emailed her back ... telling her that I was Anthony's pregnant wife. She must have been who Bob was talking about.

Anthony arrived within the hour.

"I have a textile denim deal with Lana's father, who is a big political guy in Russia. This is a very important business deal and you are ruining it!" he screamed and slapped me in the face.

Lana *was* from Russia. She was petite, blonde, and very pretty. She lived and worked at a resort in Cancun, Mexico, and her social media photos showed her and her wealthy family traveling all over the world to exotic places.

Anthony lived multiple lives. And somehow, he was able to compartmentalize each one and keep his lies straight for a long time. Since Anthony lacked empathy, he never felt guilt when he betrayed me. I realize today Anthony lacked object consistency. When I was out of sight, I was out of mind. Although when I was with him, and he wanted or needed something, he made me believe I was the center of his world.

Living with my parents was very stressful; I often felt tired and moody ... yet I felt safe. I could tell they were trying to accept Anthony and were excited about becoming grandparents. But I couldn't turn my mind off; I was constantly thinking about Anthony's other women. *Was Anthony still talking to Vicki and Betty?* I never knew.

Anthony celebrated the holidays that year at my parents' house, but only stayed overnight on Christmas Eve. He told me it was easier to stay closer to the flooded house and restaurant, which were about thirty minutes away. He said it was too much of an "inconvenience."

One morning around six, I was on my way to work and decided to stop by the trailer. I pulled into the driveway, got out of my car, and knocked on the door. There was no answer, so I knocked again, seeing his truck in the driveway. Anthony eventually opened the door and stepped outside, refusing to let me in. It was still dark, but I could tell he was very upset that I showed up without calling first. He yelled at me to go to work, and I realized he had another girl inside the trailer. I couldn't see her, but his behavior and urgency in pushing me away and not letting me inside made it obvious.

Shortly after, Anthony began sharing his fantasies of me being with other women and him. Every time we had sex, he pressured me, insisting that he wanted it to happen. He promised that if I complied, he would stay with me every night and we would buy a new house together before the baby arrived. Narcissists often use sex as a tool of manipulation rather than a form of intimacy, which can lead to strange behaviors in the bedroom, like Anthony's constant desire for threesomes. A narcissist thinks only of their own satisfaction in the bedroom, dictating everything to maximize their pleasure without considering their partner's needs. Anthony used sex as his primary tool for manipulation and control, leaving me trapped in a web of emotional turmoil.

After constant nagging and pressure from Anthony, I reluctantly agreed to his request. Being pregnant, I couldn't resort to getting drunk to numb my feelings. The mere thought of it made me feel instantly disgusted. Anthony convinced Natasha that participating was my idea and that it was essential to keep me happy until the baby was born. Natasha later revealed to me that their plan was to leave the country together and take the baby from me. Anthony had painted me as a crazy person to her, telling her that it was necessary for them to marry and that it was their special secret.

Anthony reserved a hotel near the restaurant. When I arrived, he was there with Natasha, who was already very drunk. She seemed reluctant and needed alcohol to tolerate what Anthony wanted. I wanted to back out, but Anthony pulled me aside.

"I love you; you are my wife, and I will do anything for you if you do this for me."

Despite my disgust and fear of making him angry, I went through with it. We all had sex and showered, and I felt utterly repulsed. It became clear that Natasha had slept with Anthony before; she seemed in love with him. She pretended not to understand much English, but she did. After about half an hour, he made us do it again, and this continued throughout the night. Infuriated, I took off my wedding ring and threw it at him. I yelled at Natasha to leave, and she ran out of the room with Anthony chasing after her. Eventually, she returned, and we all lay down on the king-size bed. She nestled in his arms while I sat up all night, wide awake, wanting to be far away from this revolting situation. Anthony often emptied his pockets of large amounts of cash before sleeping. *Why didn't I just take the money and drive far away?*

In the morning, Anthony told me to drive Natasha back to her apartment above the restaurant. The car ride was awkward until Natasha started talking, in perfect English. We both apologized, but I was exhausted and just wanted to escape from everyone. "Future faking" is a cunning manipulation technique used by narcissists to get what they want from their partners.

Unfortunately, Anthony continued to beg for experiences like this with him and Natasha. And if I didn't do what he asked, he began threatening to leave me.

"If you don't keep doing this, I will have more girlfriends that you won't know about and once the baby is born, and I will take her from you."

This continued until I was eight months pregnant. I feared he would take our baby, like he so easily took everything else away from me. I started to get used to doing these acts with Natasha and Anthony so much that Anthony and I never had sex together by ourselves.

"You are my wife and Natasha is my toy," he said.

It was a very sick and disturbing game that I wished and prayed would change.

Anthony received two substantial checks from the flood insurance claims. With the money, he bought his mom a house. I was about to give birth to our baby, and we didn't have our own house. Meanwhile, the restaurant was almost fully restored.

At this time, I was busy planning my baby shower. Anthony allowed me to organize it, making me feel like he cared and wanted to celebrate our daughter with family and friends. However, I realized he only permitted these parties to show off his restaurant and expensive cars, creating the illusion of a rich, successful lifestyle. It was all about enhancing Anthony's image.

Determined to make my baby shower perfect, I crafted all the decorations and planned the menu. My mom helped by purchasing all the decorations, favors, and desserts, as Anthony refused to let me pay for anything. We held the shower at the restaurant. I worked hard, cleaning and decorating the day before. All my friends from work and family came to celebrate; it was a wonderful sunny day. It started out extremely rushed because Anthony liked to wait until the last minute for everything. My friends from work arrived early but Anthony had nothing ready, not even drinks. In front of my friends, he started to yell.

"Stop talking! Hurry up and put food trays together now!"

I could tell that they were uncomfortable because he didn't even introduce himself.

After the shower was over, it was time to drive back to my parent's house. It was an enjoyable day and I loved seeing my family and friends. We loaded up my car and Anthony did not want me to stay around and help clean up. Instead, he pushed me out the door as fast as he could. It seemed the shower was an annoyance but that he did it to receive gifts. Natasha walked down the stairs at that moment, and into the middle of the argument Anthony and I were having. He grabbed my hair and started to hit me in the face with the back of his hand, because I had asked why he didn't want me to stay and help clean up. Natasha screamed for him to stop, but he wouldn't. So, she grabbed his arms and tried to pull him off me. Eventually, he backed off and I walked to my car. Natasha followed me out and asked if I was okay.

At the time, I wondered if she was also getting abused too. Later I learned she was hit, slapped, and pushed around too, but she wouldn't leave because Anthony owed her money. She had wanted to send money back to her family in Ukraine but stayed because she believed Anthony was her boyfriend—they had plans for marriage.

Anthony later told me that he had purchased a log cabin for us two hours north of Hershey. Instead of buying a house, he bought a summer cabin located near a big lake where we could take our boat out. The cabin was nice, with all wood floors and walls, a large primary suite, an open kitchen, and a living room with a view up to the second-floor loft. It needed some work and Anthony's plan was to renovate the entire place. He never discussed it with me; he simply informed me that he had bought it. I later learned Natasha had already been up to it many times; he had promised her that it was *their* special summer home.

Living with my parents had become more stressful. They were understandably worried about me being pregnant in a toxic marriage. They saw that Anthony was still treating me poorly and noticed he wasn't staying with me or making any attempts to find a house for us. I became upset with my parents constantly asking questions and urging me to stand up to him. They didn't know how severe the abuse was, I hid it well. I still desperately wanted ... needed ... to believe that Anthony would change after the baby was born. I still believed change was possible, and that there *had* to be some good in him.

Anthony's mom had not yet moved into her new house that he bought for her in Lancaster. He told me I could move in there to have less stress from living with my parents. He wanted me away from them because he didn't want them to put ideas into my head. So, I packed up and drove to the house in Lancaster. When I arrived, there was no furniture in it.

"Where am I supposed to sleep?" I asked.

"Sleep on the floor," he said, as he threw a blanket and pillow at me. He said it in such a way that I was stupid for not thinking it myself.

"I have to go to work." He left without kissing me goodbye.

There was no food, drinks, television, or even heat in the house. It was cold, and I only had a blanket and pillow. I slept about an hour that night, before a 12-hour shift on a busy trauma unit. It was a horrible decision to leave my parent's house, but at the time I felt like I couldn't go back. I slept on the cold floor for over a week until he brought any furniture. I asked if he was going to stay there too, and he shook his head.

"No, this is too far from the restaurant." Meaning, he had to stay close to Natasha.

I put everything for the baby together myself ... the toys, crib, bouncer, and rocking chair. Anthony's mom later moved into the house, and we became roommates. The living arrangement was supposed to be temporary, but it was a nice house in a good neighborhood with a park nearby in walking distance. I continued to decorate the baby's room with a baby jungle animal theme and hung up all her clothes.

One rainy April night, Anthony's mom asked if I wanted have dinner at his brother's house with his wife and son. We ate cooked eggplant parmesan, and afterwards sat in the living room to watch television. I started to have contractions that began to get closer together. I quickly realized I was going into labor. I called Anthony and he said he would us at the hospital, which was forty-five minutes away. I called my parents, and they were on their way too. His mom dropped me off at the entrance and Anthony was already there waiting. This was a surprise because he was never on time for anything. He made me get into a wheelchair and pushed me upstairs to the third floor to labor and delivery. He recorded a video of me with his phone as we went up the elevator.

He was very excited to meet our little girl, Angelina.

··· Chapter Six

The labor and delivery room we were assigned to had blue reclining chairs by the windows next to my hospital bed for family. I had the view of the front of the hospital and could see rain pouring down and cars driving by. It was a small room, but my parents, Anthony's mom and Anthony spent the night with me. I had an epidural placed by anesthesia and was able to rest from the back labor pains the rest of the night. The following morning, the doctor checked my cervix dilation and accidentally broke my water. So, I had to start pushing.

Anthony held my hand and stayed by my side with every contraction. After six very long hours of just pushing, they were about to take me to another room to do a cesarean section procedure. I pushed a few more times and Angelina was born on April 23, 2012, at 12:09PM. Anthony was there in the labor and delivery room the entire time. He cut her cord and helped the nurse clean her. She was placed on my chest and let out a cry. One of the best days of my life was the day I held Angelina after giving birth.

Soon after, Anthony left me in the delivery room and went back to wherever he was staying to shower and sleep. He didn't wait to make sure that Angelina and I were settled into our room. My parents stayed the night in the hospital while I was in labor but also stayed until we got situated in our room. He never asked if I needed anything, instead, he was in a hurry to leave. That evening, I rested in my room with Angelina. She had the most beautiful big brown eyes, olive skin, and a full head of dark hair. She looked like a delicate little angel. It was just the two of us alone and it was so special looking into her eyes. I was beyond ecstatic to finally meet her; she made me a mother. I held her in my arms and never wanted to put her down.

The next morning, the door abruptly opened to my room and Anthony and Natasha walked in ... like they were a couple coming to visit. The quiet peaceful moment Angelina and I had been sharing was over. The last person I wanted to see was Natasha, but I was too tired to fight so I bit my lip and delt with her presence. She was dressed in a tight short skirt and high heels, like she was going out. And Anthony appeared rested, freshly showered, and shaved. Natasha asked if she could hold Angelina, and they left about fifteen minutes later. Anthony didn't show any love or affection towards me or Angelina—he didn't even hold his daughter.

The following day, Angelina and I were discharged from the hospital, and Anthony drove us back to the house in Lancaster. Anthony's mom did not help, instead, she overbearingly tried to tell me how to do everything. The weather was pleasant and warm most days, so we often went on walks to get outside into the sunshine.

The house needed a lot of small repairs that Anthony said he would take care of. Anthony brought Natasha to help him work. She arrived with Anthony wearing short shorts, belly shirts, and a full face of makeup. He paraded Natasha in front of his mom and I. Anthony's mom had family cookouts at her home and Anthony brought Natasha like she was his girlfriend. His mom was very annoyed by this. I could tell his other family members were also uncomfortable with his behavior, but no one ever said anything.

"You need to fix yourself up, wear more makeup, and do your hair nice," Anthony's mom told me, two weeks after giving birth. "You know, he doesn't really like that stage."

Over the following weeks, Anthony brought Natasha to the house with him every day. While he buried himself in his work, Natasha lounged beside the pool. The sight of her jarred against the tension that simmered within the house. Anthony's mother was visibly displeased with the way he had taken over the renovations, making unilateral decisions without her input. Until one day, she expressed her frustrations openly, saying that she wanted a different place to live.

Soon Natasha also left ... to return to Ukraine. Her departure was such a breath of fresh air for me, a lifting of a suffocating weight. Yet, this relief was short-lived. Anthony's mother found a new place for herself just ten minutes away, leaving me alone in the house. The silence that followed her move was deafening. I had always found her presence annoying, her constant hovering and sharp comments grating on my nerves. But now, the realization hit me like a tidal wave. Her presence, as irritating as it was, had been a shield. With her gone, Anthony's temper had no barriers once again.

That summer, I went to the cabin a few times. It was my sanctuary, nestled near a tranquil lake surrounded by a picturesque landscape that always brought me peace. It was a place where the world seemed to slow down, and I could lose myself in the beauty of nature. Unfortunately, those precious visits were rare and tainted by the demands of work rather than relaxation.

One weekend, Anthony decided we should go up to the cabin with his father. He painted a picture of a fun, carefree weekend, just to show him the new cabin. We drove up together, the car filled with an anticipation that felt almost tangible. But even as we arrived and settled in, the weight of my responsibilities loomed over me. We stayed the night, and the next morning, as we packed up to leave, I heard Anthony in the bathroom, talking on the phone. His voice was low, but his words cut through the air like a knife.

"I bet your parents can't wait to meet me. I can't wait to come see you. I miss you so much," he said. My heart sank instantly; I knew he was speaking to Natasha.

I pushed open the bathroom door, my body trembling with a mix of anger and betrayal.

"I heard you," I said, my voice shaking. "I heard you talking about visiting Natasha."

Anthony hung up the phone, his face morphing into a mask of condescension.

"You're crazy," he spat. "You're hearing things."

Every fiber of my being knew he was lying, but his words made me waver. The gaslighting had taken its toll, making me doubt my own reality.

"I'm not crazy!" My voice echoing through the room. "I heard you clearly talking about visiting Natasha!"

Narcissistic gaslighting is a cruel form of emotional abuse, designed to make the victim question their sanity and instincts. Looking back, I realize how deeply it had affected me. Anthony's constant accusations of me being "crazy" had me frequently questioning myself, asking, "Am I crazy?" or "Did I really hear that?" His repetitive gaslighting instilled such a deep sense of confusion, forcing me to rely on him and feeding his sense of power and superiority.

Suddenly, Anthony started walking towards me, his eyes burning with rage. He pushed me down onto the floor, his hands yanking at my hair with such force that he pulled out chunks. I screamed, the pain and fear mingling in a gut-wrenching cry. His father heard me and came running into the room.

"Stop," his father said calmly, as if this was a regular occurrence.

Anthony turned to his father, his voice cold and commanding.

"Go wait in the car."

To my horror, his father obeyed without question, retreating as if nothing had happened. Angelina sat in her car seat in the living room, blissfully unaware of the chaos unfolding around her. The cabin, once my haven, had become a battleground, leaving me more isolated and broken than ever. Anthony grabbed Angelina's pack and play crib in our bedroom and threw it down the stairs and it broke. Anthony yelled at everyone to get in the truck, and we drove away. We stopped at the gas station down the street. I was still crying and told his father how sad I was about what happened. His father turned around from the front seat.

"You met him this way so don't expect him to change."

He didn't even ask if I was okay. He turned back around in his seat and continued to look out the window like nothing had happened.

The rest of the summer, Angelina and I created our own little sanctuary in the park. Every day that Anthony was absent felt like a breath of fresh air, a fleeting moment of peace in an otherwise turbulent existence. Though I never felt entirely at ease, those days without him were like small pockets of joy amidst a storm. Angelina and I spent countless hours walking to the park, her tiny hand clasped in mine. We played on the playgrounds, her laughter ringing through the air like a melody. The library became our second home, a place where stories came alive and children's classes offered a brief escape from reality. We packed our simple peanut butter and jelly sandwiches and had mini picnics under the shade of large oak trees, savoring the calmness of those moments.

But every time Anthony returned home, the peace shattered. There was always something I had done wrong in his eyes—a crumb on the floor, a smudge on the stove. His anger flared up, consuming the air around him, and he would storm out as quickly as he had arrived. His perpetual bad mood loomed over me, a dark cloud I could never escape. I tried so hard to be perfect, but perfection was a moving target I could never reach.

One day, a letter addressed to Anthony arrived in the mail. It looked like a passport. I called him to let him know, and he confirmed it was indeed a passport he had applied for. Confusion gnawed at me—why did he need a passport when neither Angelina nor I had one? A part of me wanted to destroy it, to prevent whatever plans he had in mind, but I couldn't bring myself to do it.

Later that summer, Anthony became unreachable for an entire week. His phone went straight to voicemail, and he ignored my emails and texts. Panic set in as each day passed without a word from him. When he finally showed up at the house late one night, he acted like nothing had happened, dismissing my frantic attempts to contact him as the actions of a crazy woman. The audacity of his indifference cut deep—no one should ever treat their wife and new baby that way.

After my twelve precious weeks with Angelina, I had to return to work. Anthony insisted that we needed a live-in nanny. He didn't want a daily babysitter or daycare; he wanted a nanny from a foreign country, someone he wouldn't have to pay much. Reluctantly, I plunged into the daunting task of finding one.

The first girl, from Brazil, was living in Philadelphia. She was kind, spoke English well, and seemed like a good fit. But Anthony had other plans. He wanted her to work at his restaurant instead. She spent the night at our house, and Anthony tried to charm her with alcohol and card games. She drank some wine but refused to play his games, seeing through his intentions. Anthony's displeasure was palpable.

He pressured me to find more candidates, and eventually, I found Elena, a 20-year-old from Kazakhstan living in New York City. She had long, dark hair, pale skin, and a quiet demeanor. She arrived in Lancaster with a friend, barely speaking any English. I introduced her to Angelina, and though she was shy, she agreed to be our live-in nanny. When Anthony arrived to meet Elena, she looked visibly uncomfortable. He never discussed her pay with me, leaving me in the dark once again. But she agreed to start within a few days, and I hoped against hope that this arrangement would bring some stability to our chaotic lives.

I didn't know this girl, and yet she was going to be living in our house. Anthony still wasn't sleeping at home, leaving me to navigate this new arrangement alone. Elena arrived a few days later, a single suitcase in her hand and an air of hopefulness about her. She told us that it was her first year in America and that she had never celebrated American holidays. Her excitement to be here was palpable, a stark contrast to the tension that hung in the air.

As a new family, I longed for moments with just Anthony, Angelina, and myself. But those moments were elusive. With Elena now living with us, Anthony insisted she accompany us everywhere, even on the shortest errands. There was never any time alone as a family, and I felt the weight of that absence deeply. I questioned Anthony about it, but our conversations circled around the issue without resolution.

Anthony orchestrated my work schedule so that I worked three consecutive days at the hospital. My shifts were grueling, from seven in the morning until seven in the evening, and I wouldn't return home until after eight at night. During those long days, Anthony and Elena spent time together, taking care of Angelina, going on day trips, and visiting his family in New York. It felt as if they were the real family, and I was just an outsider looking in. When I worked weekends, I sometimes didn't see my daughter for six days straight, a heart-wrenching reality.

Anthony's visits to our house became more frequent with Elena's presence. One evening, not long after she started caring for Angelina, Anthony decided that Elena should drink alcohol and play cards. I knew what was coming—he wanted to indulge his sick fantasy again. He promised that if I convinced her to play along, he would stay overnight more often and refrain from finding another girlfriend. Reluctantly, I tried to persuade Elena, who revealed she had never had a boyfriend or slept with a man. This only fueled Anthony's desire, his manipulation becoming more apparent.

Elena used to take the train back to New York to stay with her girlfriend, but now she stayed with us more often. On the days I worked, Anthony would take Angelina and Elena to the cabin for construction work, staying overnight frequently. It was a two-hour drive, and he claimed it was easier to stay there. I was expected to be okay with this arrangement, but I wasn't. Then, out of the blue, I started receiving phone calls from Natasha. I had almost forgotten about her.

"What car are you driving right now?" was the first question she asked. I told her I was driving the Mercedes. I explained that nothing had changed—I was still driving the same car, living in the same house, and married to the same man. Her outrage was immediate. She revealed that Anthony had visited her that summer, met her entire family, and told them he was going to marry her. He had been promising her a divorce from me. She let out a frustrated sigh and hung up. I sat down and cried, confusion and betrayal flooding my heart. I had thought Anthony was done with her, that she had moved on with her life.

The next time I saw Anthony, he was already furious. I confronted him about Natasha, but he didn't need to hear my questions. He grabbed me by the hair and dragged me into the downstairs bathroom, slamming my head against the wall, leaving yet another mark that would be my fault. He then dragged me to the bedroom, pressing his fingers into my eyes and pressure points behind my ears, boasting about his jujitsu skills and the pain they could cause. The pain was unbearable, and I wished I could pass out to escape it.

Anthony threw me onto the bed, suffocating me with a pillow until I saw white dots and could no longer fight back. His screams filled the room, calling me stupid, asking if I had a brain. I couldn't catch my breath. He flipped me over, tore off my clothes, and raped me. My pleas for him to stop only made him angrier. He slapped my face and yelled.

"Stop crying! You look ugly when you cry!"

I was powerless, my body weak from the assault. I realized then that this was a violent phase in the cycle of sexual abuse from a narcissist. Once we reached this stage, sex was no longer an expression of mutual love or commitment. It became an act of intimidation, control, domination, power, torture, and terror. Anthony's actions were criminal, and I was the unfortunate victim. The FBI defines rape as penetration without the consent of the victim, and that day, I was undeniably a victim.

Natasha continued to contact me, or I would reach out to her, driven by a mix of curiosity and desperation. Our conversations would sometimes stretch for hours, a strange camaraderie forming between us. Despite the odd friendship developing, every time we spoke, Anthony found out. Our anger would eventually boil over, leading to confrontations with him. Each confrontation ended the same way: with me bearing the brunt of his rage.

The bruises on my head never had a chance to fade, a new one appearing almost every other day. Anthony's steel-toe work boots became instruments of torture, kicking me until I fell. He would then drag me by my hair or arms into the bedroom, leaving carpet burns on my elbows from being pulled so many times. Once there, he would pin me down with his knees, yanking my hair so hard that my neck bent backward. My body ached so much that even a hot shower or daily doses of Motrin couldn't dull the pain. Dressing for work each morning became an arduous task, and any visible bruises had to be meticulously covered with makeup.

I started to notice Elena's growing interest in Anthony. When I asked her to help more around the house or take care of Angelina, she began to ignore me. I brought this up with Anthony, but he defended Elena, claiming I was asking too much of her. Her responsibilities included cleaning up after Angelina, doing her laundry, and keeping the kitchen tidy, yet the house often remained a mess. Anthony's threats became more frequent, insisting that if I didn't initiate these degrading card games with Elena, he would find someone else to sleep with. I feared him, feared being alone, and most of all, feared losing Angelina. Unbeknownst to me, he was already promising Elena that he would divorce me and marry her.

Elena began to refuse to watch Angelina unless it was at the cabin. Anthony told me she didn't want to be near me or speak to me, and that I needed to apologize to her. Reluctantly, I texted her an apology, saying I was sorry for asking too much and that my main concern was Angelina's safety. She resumed watching Angelina at the house but treated me with cold indifference, refusing to speak or even look at me.

One night, Anthony insisted we drink alcohol and get drunk. I complied, but this time he started having sex with Elena in front of me. I attempted to pull her away from him. Anthony retaliated by throwing me to the floor, pressing my face into the carpet, and beating me with his boot. Elena screamed for him to stop, and he did, but the damage was done. This was the first time she had witnessed his brutality. Soon after, Elena's attitude toward me worsened, treating me as if I were Anthony's servant. She talked back to me, confident in her belief that she was going to replace me. Anthony took my Mercedes away after I discovered he was still talking to Natasha and now sleeping with Elena. I felt trapped in a nightmare, unable to confide in my coworkers or friends. The thought of revealing that I was forced to have sex with my husband and the nanny, or that he constantly threatened to leave me, was too humiliating.

One of my days off, Anthony and Elena arrived at the house unannounced in his white Mercedes. Despite making payments on the car, I had no money left for myself. Elena went straight to the guest room and closed the door, while Angelina napped upstairs. Anthony came downstairs to where I was doing laundry, began kissing me, and told me he loved me. He apologized for everything but insisted I needed to listen to him. He claimed his relationship with Elena was all a game to get her to work for free and that I needed to pretend she was my girlfriend.

He picked up a curling iron from my dresser, tied the cord around my wrists, and told me to sit on the bed. Exhausted and filled with dread, I complied. He went upstairs to Elena's room, leaving me naked and bound. After a long time, I managed to free myself and started to quietly go upstairs. He heard me, rushed out of her room, and dragged me back downstairs. He began having sex with me, ignoring my pleas to stop.

Anthony then grabbed my upper body, pushed me to the ground, and took out real police handcuffs, showing me the key, he alone possessed. He handcuffed me to the bottom post of the bed, asserting his control. I was on my knees, naked and terrified, unable to escape. My cries for him to stop fell on deaf ears, leaving me trapped and powerless in an unimaginable nightmare.

He ascended the stairs slowly, a predator savoring the anticipation. When he opened the door to Elena's room, I felt a pit in my stomach. Minutes stretched like hours before he returned, his eyes gleaming with a twisted satisfaction. He began to strip me of my clothes, his hands rough and unyielding. Naked and vulnerable, I lay there as he tied my wrists with the curling iron cord. He kissed me, a mockery of intimacy, before leaving me to rejoin Elena upstairs.

Time seemed to slow, each second filled with dread. The house was eerily silent except for the occasional creak of the floorboards above. Desperation gave me strength, and I managed to free my hands. I crept upstairs, my heart pounding in my chest. But he heard me. He burst out of Elena's room and grabbed me by the wrist, dragging me back downstairs. He resumed his assault, ignoring my pleas for mercy. He pushed me to the ground, his grip bruising my upper body. With a flourish, he produced real police handcuffs, locking my wrists to the bottom post of the bed.

"These are real," he said, dangling the key in front of my face.

I begged him to stop, tears streaming down my face, but he was unmoved. Naked and handcuffed, I knelt by the bed, utterly powerless.

Anthony left me there, my mind a whirlwind of fear and humiliation. Moments later, he returned with Elena, who was also naked. He pushed her onto the bed, forcing me to watch as he violated her from behind.

"Stop!" I screamed, my voice breaking.

He looked at me with a cruel smile.

"You like this, don't you?" he taunted.

"Please, stop! This is not what I want!" I cried, my voice raw with desperation.

Elena turned to me, her face twisted with malice.

"Shut up, you stupid bitch!" she spat.

Anthony commanded her to get on the bed with him, their sordid act continuing. She looked down at me, her eyes cold and mocking, and laughed. Rage boiled within me, and I lifted the bed with all my might, my wrists burning as the handcuffs cut into my flesh. My scream echoed through the room, raw and primal. Anthony finally stopped, his expression one of shock and annoyance.

My wrists were bleeding, the pain searing. I was shaking uncontrollably, unable to catch my breath. Elena smirked one last time before retreating upstairs. Anthony retrieved the key and unlocked the cuffs, his face a mask of contempt.

"I thought that's what you wanted," he sneered. "You know deep down you liked it." His words were a dagger to my soul. I had never smiled, never encouraged him. I had screamed and cried, desperate for it all to end.

He dressed and kissed my forehead, a grotesque parody of affection, before leaving with Elena in his white Mercedes. I was left alone, shattered and traumatized. The thought of calling the police crossed my mind, but Anthony's threats loomed large. He boasted of his connections with local authorities, making it clear that any attempt to seek help would be futile.

I took a hot shower, the water mingling with my tears. Angelina slept peacefully in her room, blissfully unaware of the horrors unfolding around her. The scars from that night were not just physical. They etched themselves into my psyche, leaving me with symptoms of post-traumatic stress disorder (PTSD). My wrists never fully healed, diagnosed with Wartenberg's Syndrome from the tight handcuffs. The pain was a constant reminder of my helplessness, a cruel souvenir of my captivity.

Weeks later, Elena reached out to me, her voice tinged with an uncharacteristic remorse. I recounted the terror of that night, and she apologized. I accepted, but trust was a bridge long burned. Anthony, ever the master manipulator, had another twisted plan. He returned home, all sweetness and affection, promising to stay overnight and professing his love. His words were hollow, a façade for his sick obsession with controlling and degrading me. The nightmare continued, each day a struggle to survive in a world where my tormentor held all the power.

Anthony's voice dripped with manipulation, telling me I would be the best wife ever if I agreed to have sex with him and Elena that night. I suspected he was feeding her the same twisted line. The night was a blur of alcohol and compliance. I did what he demanded, my actions a desperate attempt to keep the peace. He stayed over that night, but by morning, he left with Elena, leaving me with a growing sense of disgust. However, his sexual obsessions had become a grim routine.

Anthony's desires were a dark abyss, filled with violent fantasies and coercion. His needs always overshadowed mine, his sense of sexual entitlement an ever-present force. Manipulation was his weapon, and he wielded it to fulfill his fantasies, exploiting me without remorse. His life was a tangled web of obsessions, from porn addiction to infidelity. Yet, despite everything, I feared his departure. He had ingrained in me the belief that I couldn't survive without him, that he would take Angelina away if he left. This fear kept me compliant, agreeing to his every whim.

Anthony's next scheme was to isolate Elena and me. I tried to warn her about what he did to Natasha, recounting the entire story. But my words fell on deaf ears; he had her under his spell. Soon, Elena stopped responding to my texts and calls, confining her interactions with Angelina to the cabin.

The year passed in a haze of pain and fear. Each week, Anthony's anger found a new target in me. I couldn't help but wonder if he abused his other girlfriends too. Natasha later told me he had tried to get physical with her, but she fought back, leaving him with a black eye. When I saw Elena, she often wore short shorts and belly shirts, much like Natasha. Bruises marred her body, silent testimonies to Anthony's violence.

We celebrated Angelina's first birthday at a restaurant. I had meticulously planned the party, wanting it to be perfect for her. Family and friends gathered; the day filled with joy. But for me, it started with chaos. Anthony, as usual, waited until the last minute to set up, leaving me to scramble while guests arrived. My friend Jess came early to help, decorating and watching Angelina. She put pigtails in Angelina's hair, making her look adorable. My sister had bought her a pink tutu birthday outfit with a pink cupcake on the shirt.

In front of everyone, Anthony began to yell and scream at me. I could see the discomfort on the faces of my friend and her mother. While his outbursts had become normal to me, others saw the reality of my situation. Despite the frightening scene, Jess stood by me, always showing up because she cared.

Angelina's birthday theme was pink sparkly ballerinas. I had made a pink smash cake with the number one on it, ballerina cupcakes with tutus, and various cute sparkly decorations and favors. Our family and friends arrived, and Angelina, ever the happy child, beamed with joy. Once the party ended, we packed up and headed home. Anthony rarely traveled with us, preferring to meet us at locations since he never stayed overnight at our home. The restaurant still needed cleaning, but Anthony told me to go home. I suspected Elena was waiting nearby. The photos from Angelina's birthday were joyful on the surface, but behind my smile was a well of fear and sadness. Pretending to be happy in front of our families was becoming increasingly difficult. I longed to fall apart and cry.

Motherhood changed me profoundly. Angelina depended on me entirely, and I lavished her with love. To protect her, I worked hard to keep Anthony happy, terrified he would turn his violence on her. Celebrations with friends and family were rare, precious moments Anthony allowed. My parents only saw Angelina on birthdays or holidays, controlled by Anthony's whims.

Despite the façade, my heart ached with the weight of our reality. Each day was a battle to protect my daughter and survive under Anthony's oppressive control.

Chapter Seven

Our family was caught in the toxic grip of a narcissistic structure, with each of us entangled in unhealthy relationships and damaging dynamics. Despite the illusion of being a family, the focus was always on satisfying Anthony's needs, often at the expense of our daughter, Angelina. For instance, Anthony demanded that his dinner be prepared before I could even think about making her bottles or food. The pressure to keep him happy was relentless, and the fear of his anger or physical outbursts in front of Angelina consumed me.

I still worry today that Angelina might bear the emotional scars of growing up with a narcissistic father. She might develop intense anxiety, PTSD, or depression, mirroring my own struggle. If deprived of proper love, she could feel as detached and estranged as I often do. To survive, she may have tried to make herself invisible, a coping mechanism that could haunt her future relationships.

Throughout the year, the abuse continued, and my body began to show the strain. Waking up at five in the morning and enduring twelve-hour shifts on a busy trauma floor at the hospital became increasingly difficult as my malnourished body ached. Recovery took longer and longer. Some nights, Anthony would come home very late, demanding sex without a care for my exhaustion. When I told him no, explaining that I had to be up early for my fourth consecutive twelve-hour shift, his rage was swift and brutal. Refusing him was met with violence. He would hit or slap me, his fury knowing no bounds. One night, he grabbed my head, yanked my hair, and slammed it against the wall repeatedly until I saw stars. Anger welled up inside me, and I began to push him away more often, a new defiance he despised. He was accustomed to my silent endurance. One brutal kick with his steel-toe work boots sent my back into spasms, the pain so intense I couldn't move. This paralysis gave him more opportunity to inflict harm, suffocating me with pillows or choking me with his hands until I seemed lifeless.

After each of these violent episodes, he would coldly declare deadly threats on my life.

"You know one of these days when we fight like this, I am going to end up killing you."

Then, as if nothing about what he had just said was deplorable would continue.

"Are you done acting up? Take your clothes off."

Forced to have sex with him, tears streamed down my cheeks. If I didn't pretend to enjoy it, he would slap me hard, especially if he saw me crying. My lack of enthusiasm was met with more violence, throwing my body to the floor, and kicking me all over again. During one particularly savage fight, he kicked me so hard in the side of my abdomen that I felt like my lung had collapsed. Struggling to catch my breath, I saw a flicker of concern in Anthony's eyes, not out of compassion, but because he feared I might need medical attention. These fights often took place in the dead of night, while Angelina slept in her bed or at the cabin with whichever nanny or girlfriend Anthony had at the time.

The facade of normalcy was crumbling, the reality of our lives hidden behind closed doors. Each day was a battle for survival, a desperate attempt to shield my daughter from the horrors of our existence. My love for Angelina was the only light in the darkness, a fragile hope that one day, we might escape this nightmare.

As soon as left, I felt the weight of the world lift momentarily, only to be replaced by an overwhelming sadness and despair. I stumbled into the bathroom, hands trembling, and turned the shower knob to the hottest setting I could bear. The steam filled the room as I sank to the floor, letting the scorching water cascade over me. The heat was a temporary distraction, a searing pain to mask the deeper wounds. Chunks of my hair slipped through my fingers, swirling down the drain along with my tears. I cried, sobbing uncontrollably, and asked God time and time again why this was happening to me. The sadness was suffocating, the depression an endless abyss. I felt utterly alone, trapped in a nightmare with no escape.

The following morning, I somehow managed to pull myself together, masking the pain. I went to work as if nothing had happened, the routine a thin veneer over my fractured reality. One of my close friends at work, who had met Anthony once and knew more than I had ever told her, noticed my discomfort. She checked my body when I confided that something felt seriously wrong. Anthony's brutal kick had fractured my ribs; there was little to be done but endure the pain with Motrin and tape. She could feel the rib clicking beneath her fingers, a grim confirmation of the damage.

I didn't have to tell her that Anthony was responsible; she already knew. She also confirmed that my nasal septum was broken. I showed up to work with bruises marring my arms and face, trying desperately to cover them with makeup. The lies spilled from my lips when coworkers asked what had happened, each fabricated story a layer of shame. It was humiliating to lie about my injuries, to hide the truth of my suffering.

One evening, we sat down to dinner, and Angelina, being a typical toddler, was fussy about her food. New tastes and textures made her resistant to eating everything on her plate. Anthony's patience snapped. He forced her to eat every bite, slapping her mouth and holding it shut until she swallowed. Her cries escalated to dry heaves, and she ended up vomiting her entire meal. This was the first time I witnessed Anthony's violence directed at our daughter, a horrifying realization that shattered me. I felt helpless and horrified, frozen by the unpredictability of his wrath.

Anthony's anger was palpable as he stood up, yelling at Angelina before storming out, slamming the front door behind him. The silence that followed was deafening. I rushed to Angelina, scooping her up and holding her tightly. Her little body trembled with sobs, and I could feel her distress. I took her to the bathroom and gently bathed her, trying to wash away the horror of what had just occurred. I held her close, whispering soothing words, desperate to comfort her and make her forget. In those moments, I made a silent vow to protect her, to find a way out of this living hell. The fear and sadness I felt were overwhelming, but my love for Angelina gave me strength. She was my reason to keep fighting, my beacon of hope amid darkness.

That summer, Anthony told me he would be spending the entire season working on construction projects at the cabin and restaurant. It was an unusual suggestion when he told me to visit my parents more often, but I seized the opportunity. Taking Angelina to my parents' place became a frequent solace, a rare escape from the suffocating grip of my life with Anthony. It was a breath of fresh air, a chance to let my guard down and let Angelina bask in the love and attention of her grandparents. When my parents proposed a week-long trip to the beach, I was elated. This would be our first real vacation together, a precious opportunity to create happy memories with my daughter.

Despite knowing Anthony was cheating on me with Elena, I found myself becoming indifferent. I craved the time away, a chance to breathe without his oppressive presence. When I approached him about the beach trip, he surprisingly agreed without hesitation. It was a rare concession, as I usually had to seek his permission for any plans I wished to make.

Throughout our beach vacation, I had to constantly check in with Anthony. His paranoia and insecurity were suffocating. He never trusted me alone, always projecting his own infidelity onto me. If I missed a call and it went to voicemail, it was a catastrophe. Anthony's narcissism drove him to accuse me of cheating, deflecting his guilt, and projecting his insecurities onto me. He thrived on confusion, minimization, and devaluation during our arguments, leaving me feeling small and powerless.

The week at the beach with my parents and Angelina flew by. My parents showered Angelina with clothes and toys, something Anthony rarely did. She delighted in the sand and the ocean, fearless in the face of the crashing waves. She wore a pink polka dot tutu swimsuit, her laughter filling the air as we splashed in the water and built sandcastles. Angelina's patience and good behavior were a testament to her sweet nature. Our dinners out were peaceful, her little face lighting up with joy. This vacation became one of my most cherished memories, a sanctuary of peace, quiet, and freedom from stress and violence. Returning home felt like stepping back into a nightmare. The abuse resumed immediately, with the constant fighting and tension wearing down my spirit and body. Every night, I began to pray for Anthony not to come home and disturb my fragile sleep. The fear of being woken and beaten was a relentless shadow over my nights, eroding my strength and resolve.

One evening, after putting Angelina to bed, another argument erupted. Desperate and cornered, I grabbed my phone and threatened to call my mom. Anthony scoffed, never believing I would go through with it. But I did. Through tears, I told my mom I wanted to come home. Anthony snatched the phone from me, trying to convince her I was crazy. I had no choice but to agree with him, reassuring my mom that everything was fine while he stood on my feet, his weight a painful reminder of my helplessness.

After hanging up, Anthony took my phone and car keys, shoving me outside and locking the door. I sat on the front porch, the minutes dragging into what felt like an eternity. When he finally let me back in, he expected a warm welcome. Instead, my anger boiled over. I slammed the front door with all my might. In a fit of rage, Anthony grabbed my head and slammed it into the stairs, blood splattered across the stairs and walls. His only concern was the carpet, as he hurried to clean up the blood with a towel before leaving the house. The physical pain was excruciating, but it was the emotional wounds that cut the deepest. That night, as I cleaned my own blood from the stairs, I felt a resolve harden within me. This couldn't be my life, and for Angelina's sake, I had to find a way out.

That fall, Anthony bought a motorcycle from a girl who had just broken up with her boyfriend. He boasted about the amazing deal he got, claiming he could sell it for more than he paid. But his financial decisions were never a part of my world; he made them unilaterally, leaving me on the periphery of our shared life.

One evening, while I was working on the trauma unit at the hospital, my phone buzzed incessantly with emails and texts from Elena. Elena and I had stopped communicating; she ignored my calls and texts after initially promising to care for our daughter. The feeling of helplessness, knowing someone else was caring for my child yet refusing to communicate with me, was one of the worst I had ever experienced. Elena's latest messages were a storm of revelations. She told me Anthony was cheating on me with another girl named Rachel—the same girl he bought the motorcycle from. Elena was visibly upset, feeling betrayed because she thought Anthony would leave me for her, a promise he had made to Natasha before her. Now, she saw him for the cheater he truly was.

Desperate for answers, I decided to call Rachel. She answered, and I explained who I was, that I was Anthony's wife, and that we had a child together. She was stunned and suggested we meet at a restaurant to talk. Rachel turned out to be kind and genuinely furious—not at me, but at Anthony. She had been dating him for just over a month, unaware of his lies. Unlike the other girls Anthony cheated on me with, Rachel's anger was directed solely at him, or maybe I was just too exhausted to care anymore.

Rachel called her ex-boyfriend, who joined us at the restaurant. We planned to confront Anthony that night when he was supposed to come over to Rachel's apartment. But he never showed. Frustrated, I drove back home and called Anthony, screaming and confronting him. He twisted the narrative, claiming Rachel was obsessed with him. His indifference to my pain was chilling; he didn't care that he was hurting me. His only concern was the motorcycle he had deceitfully acquired. Anthony continued his cycle of deceit, moving from one girl to the next without remorse.

His relationship with Elena deteriorated; he began complaining about her to me, criticizing her cleaning and even making her paint the garage at the cabin. She seemed to be getting hurt frequently, and one day, he called to tell me she had fallen off a ladder while painting. He even asked if he should get her medical attention. A few weeks later, Elena moved back to Kazakhstan. My attempts to reach out to her were met with curt replies. She wanted nothing to do with Anthony or me ever again. Anthony later admitted he had forced her to return home because he was tired of her.

The holidays that year were a nightmare. To this day, I dread the holiday season. Early in our relationship, we split our time between my parents' and his family's houses. But now, we only went to his family's gatherings. Thanksgiving Day was particularly awful. Anthony arrived home late, and we had already been arguing. Every time we visited his family, he treated me horribly, ignoring me, and demanding I serve him. It seemed that he wanted his family to see that we were not getting along.

That afternoon, as I prepared Angelina and packed the food I had baked, Anthony stormed in, yelling. Sick of the constant mistreatment, I told him to go without me, never expecting him to take Angelina and leave me alone on Thanksgiving. But he did. As he took Angelina outside to the truck, I followed, shouting that she should stay with me. He got into the truck, and as I stood behind it, he backed up and hit me. The impact wasn't enough to knock me over, but it hurt. Defeated, I walked back into the house, crying.

I spent that Thanksgiving alone, feeling utterly abandoned. Anthony returned late that evening, demanding I get dressed to go to his aunt's house. Exhausted from crying and with little food at home, I complied. When we arrived, his aunt asked how work at the hospital was, a lie Anthony had concocted to explain my absence. His cousin approached me, asking if we were separated. I told her we were still married. Anthony had already begun spreading lies to ease the path for his future plans. Christmas was no different. I felt like an outsider in his family, isolated by the lies he told them. I was lonely, but my priority was ensuring Angelina's happiness.

Once again, we were without a nanny for Angelina. I was tired of meeting Anthony's impossible specifications and his games with the nannies. I eventually found a local college girl looking for a side job. She watched Angelina at our house while I worked. Anthony never bothered her, probably because she wasn't his type. But he didn't pay her well, and after a few months, she stopped watching Angelina. As I looked back on that tumultuous time, I realized how deeply entrenched I was in Anthony's web of lies and deceit. But for Angelina, I continued to endure, hoping for a brighter future for both of us.

Anthony owed a lot of people money. One day, the babysitter opened the door to find the sheriff standing there. The officer handed her legal papers from a lawyer suing Anthony for unpaid bills, which made Anthony furious. I suspect he pushed the babysitter to quit after that. He then told me that we no longer needed a nanny or babysitter for Angelina, claiming he would watch her himself. I found it hard to believe he could manage a two-year-old while trying to work.

It was a bitter winter evening when Anthony asked me to pick up one of his workers from the train station near our house. I dutifully went and picked up a girl named Sophia. I had no idea she was another one of Anthony's Ukrainian girlfriends. Angelina recognized her immediately.

"Sophia!"

She was polite, young—maybe eighteen—and beautiful, with long brown hair and a slender frame. I brought her back to our house, thinking she would stay overnight, until Anthony picked her up the next day for work. That evening, Sophia watched television with us, and played with Angelina. I showed her to the spare room, and we all went to sleep. Throughout the night, Anthony kept texting me, urging me to get Sophia drunk and coax her into "playing games" with us later. I ignored him, tired of his endless games and constant talk about wanting to have sex with me and these young girls.

The next morning, Angelina and I were up early, making breakfast. We waited for Sophia to join us, but she never came out. Hours passed, and it was almost noon. She stayed in her room until she heard the front door open. It was Anthony. She came running down the stairs to greet him with a huge smile on her face. My heart sank. Here we go again, I thought, another one of Anthony's girlfriends. After they left, I picked up my phone and searched for Sophia on social media. I found her on a European platform, seeing pictures of her on our boat at the cabin, posing in our cars, and even on Anthony's back in the water, both of them holding alcoholic drinks and smiling like they were on vacation.

Determined to get answers, I searched for her on Skype and called her. She answered but struggled with English, suggesting I text her instead. I explained who I was—Anthony's wife. It was a conversation I found myself having far too often, one I should never have had to have. My head was clouded with confusion and hurt. Sophia became angry and confronted Anthony, just as I did. He beat me for questioning him about her. He tried to keep us from talking, feeding us both lies. He told Sophia he would leave me for her and told me he was using her for cheap labor, just like the other girls.

Sophia and I continued to talk, but it was a strained relationship. She became upset with me, insisting I leave her boyfriend alone while I fought for my marriage. Living far from my family and isolated from work, I felt utterly alone. My friends from work often invited me out, but I had to decline because Anthony wouldn't allow it. I convinced Anthony to sell our house in Lancaster so we could be closer to my work and family. He wanted his money back, so he had an interest in selling the house. I didn't care where we lived; the plan was to stay in the farmhouse until we found our final home. But that was just another lie. Anthony promised that if I did as he asked, we would have our forever house sooner.

The week before New Year's Day, I had some time off work. During those days, I received only a few terse texts from Anthony. The day before New Year's Eve, he called, claiming he was in the hospital after having a stroke.

"I just had a stroke, and you are the one who caused it," he said.

He was angry, blaming me for his stress and subsequent health scare.

"You want me to die, and you caused me so much stress that I had a stroke," he continued, "I can't be around anyone who stresses me out."

Anthony was using guilt-tripping, a manipulative tactic to control and dominate me emotionally. He made me feel responsible for his health decline, positioning himself as the victim. I felt terrible but then realized he was speaking normally, which made me doubt the severity of his alleged stroke. The nurse in me knew that if he really had a stroke, he wouldn't be talking so coherently.

On New Year's Eve, Anthony came to the house, claiming he would stay with Angelina and me for the holiday. His mom stopped by to see him too. Anthony handed me his discharge instructions; all the scans and tests were negative. He hadn't had a stroke. The papers indicated high blood pressure, likely due to stress—probably from his frequent bouts of anger and screaming. Despite the evidence, Anthony insisted he'd had a stroke. When I gave him my nursing opinion, he stood up, screamed at me, and left the house. Every disagreement from then on ended with him yelling.

"I'm going to have another stroke, and I'm not arguing with you. I'm leaving."

This was the silent treatment, a punishment tactic employed by guilt trippers. Anthony used it to withdraw emotionally, making me feel isolated and desperate for his attention and forgiveness.

My birthday is also in January, and I always loved to celebrate birthdays. Anthony, on the other hand, did not care to celebrate anything unless it involved him. I told him that I wanted to go out to eat with just him, Angelina, and I. I didn't think this would be too much to ask of him. He arrived at the house in Lancaster in his truck and beeped the horn. I walked outside thinking it was just going to be the three of us.

There was another young girl maybe twenty years old in the front seat with long brown hair dressed the same as all the other young girls wearing a short dress and high heels in the cold. I had never met her before. I was angry that he brought another girl with him. I looked at her and pointed for her to get in the back seat. I was not going to be treated like that on my birthday. She got out of the car and went to sit in the backseat. Anthony was surprised that I did that, and he rolled his eyes. I introduced myself and she said her name was Ethel. She was from Hungary, and like all the other young girls, she spoke very little English. We went to eat at a steakhouse that Anthony picked out. I did not have a choice where I wanted to go for my birthday. Ethel started to take care of Angelina by cutting her food and helping her eat. Angelina smiled at her. Right then I noticed that Angelina also knew her well. Ethel must have been taking care of Angelina for a while because she seemed comfortable around her. I knew it had to be confusing for her to have different babysitters every few months. Having so many different babysitters may be a minor concern, but it had to be hard on a child not having a solid family structure at home.

After we finished at the restaurant, Anthony stopped at the liquor store and picked up a case of wine coolers. My stomach sank because I knew what was going to happen next. I didn't want to be a divorced single mother and I didn't want to be alone, so I always just did whatever Anthony told me to do. My thoughts at the time were that there was no way I would be able to survive without Anthony. I did what he told me, or he threatened to take away my daughter, car, job, or beat me. Anytime I talked to Anthony about leaving he got physically abusive towards me. I was never able to comprehend that there were other options, especially the option of leaving. I understand now that a victim such as myself has reasons for staying with their abusers that are extremely complex, and, in most cases, are based on the reality that their abuser will follow through with threats they have used to keep them trapped. I had thought to myself many times that Anthony was quite capable of killing me, or hurting my daughter. I often felt that our relationship was mixed with good times, love, and hope along with the manipulation, intimidation, and fear that kept me staying. I had a huge fear of losing the means to support myself because Anthony had drowned me in debt, as I was not in control of my own money. Anthony also told me that he could easily plant drugs in my car and have one of his police officer friends come and arrest me anytime he wanted.

"After I do that, you will get arrested, and then you will lose your job and Angelina. Not even your parents will want you back because you will be a failure."

He knew how important my daughter and job were to me. There was too much fear and dependence of Anthony.

When we arrived back to the house, I put Angelina to bed and Anthony was excited to start drinking and playing his card games. I did what Anthony wanted and we ended up playing his games and having sex. It did not seem like this was the first time Ethel and Anthony had slept together. Of course, this worried me. Anthony and Ethel left the house and he lied and told me that he was dropping her off at her husband's house. She lied and told me that she was married and living with her husband who also worked for Anthony. Little did I know that Ethel and Anthony had been sharing an apartment together. I was disgusted with myself, so I showered and cried to myself to sleep. That was not how I wanted to spend my birthday.

That winter was a dark time for me. Anthony still came to the house late at night, demanding sex. The weight of stress and fear crushed me; I couldn't comply. One night, I mustered the courage to say "no." Anthony's face twisted in rage. He took off his belt and began to hit me with it. Each strike burned my skin, leaving red welts on my back and stomach. The pain was excruciating, but the emotional numbness that followed was worse. When he left after these beatings, a wave of depression washed over me. Sometimes, I would run into the bathroom to cry, hiding my tears from Angelina. The thought of ending my life crossed my mind many times, especially when I felt isolated and alone. But I couldn't do it; I knew it would shatter Angelina's life. So, I wore a mask of smiles, trying to hide the darkness within.

That following spring, we sold the house in Lancaster and moved into a farmhouse in Hershey. The commute to my job was just ten minutes, which I loved. Despite its small size, the farmhouse was manageable and sat on almost seven acres of beautiful land. We put a lot of work into the property, but Anthony still rarely stayed overnight with Angelina and me, even though the restaurant was only fifteen minutes away.

However, being closer to work allowed me to spend more time with my friends. I started to grow closer to Morgan, a colleague from my unit. Surprisingly, Anthony didn't seem to mind me going out with friends, likely because he was juggling multiple girlfriends. Morgan needed a part-time job, so I suggested she work for Anthony and perhaps spy on him to uncover what really went on at his restaurant. Anthony had forbidden me from visiting the restaurant, claiming he needed to open it occasionally to keep the liquor license active. Morgan agreed to work a Friday night to find out the truth.

After her shift, Morgan called me and described a quiet evening with only a few of Anthony's friends present. She stood behind the bar, making drinks and witnessed Anthony handling a lot of cash. Everyone eventually moved to another room for about an hour before she was paid and went home. The next day, Anthony angrily accused Morgan of getting drunk and trying to have sex with him, calling her a slut, and warning me to stay away from her. Confused and conditioned to believe Anthony, I doubted Morgan.

Upset, Morgan confronted me, devastated that I believed Anthony's lies. She came to my house, knocking on the door and asking to talk to me, but I refused to answer. I called Anthony for help, and he called the police on her. The officers told Morgan never to return, making Anthony look like a hero. He continued to warn me against Morgan, painting her as unstable and dangerous.

At work, Morgan and I eventually reconciled. She understood the control and abuse I was under and chose to help me rather than walk away. She tried to open my eyes to Anthony's manipulation, but I was still blind. Anthony consumed every part of my life. When I felt scared or in trouble, he was the one I turned to, despite being the source of my pain.

Since moving to the farmhouse, Anthony rarely stayed overnight or kept his belongings there. He claimed to live at the restaurant, never allowing me to see where he slept. Exhausted from work and maintaining the property, I didn't have the energy to care. Anthony admitted that Ethel was watching Angelina while I worked, and she often accompanied him. Ethel was friendly and wanted to spend time with me, making plans for shopping trips with Angelina. Little did I know what she and Anthony were plotting.

In March, Morgan and I attended a friend's baby shower. On our way back, we planned to stop by the farmhouse to ride her four-wheeler that we stored for her, but it wouldn't start. As Morgan headed to her car, she noticed Anthony's truck in the driveway, unlocked. Suspicious, Morgan suggested we look inside. Despite my reservations, we found Ethel's clothes, sunglasses, and makeup in the truck. A stack of cash lay in the driver's side door. Morgan's eyes widened, but I insisted we leave everything as it was before taking Ethel's Ray-Ban sunglasses and putting them in my purse.

Within minutes, Anthony arrived, driving fast. He must have known there was something in the truck he didn't want me to see. Morgan confronted him about her four-wheeler, but he ignored her. She left, upset, and Anthony soon followed without a word.

Later that evening, Anthony and Ethel returned to pressure wash the house. Watching Ethel closely, I noticed the way she looked at Anthony was not how a worker looked at their boss. Something was definitely going on. Following Morgan's advice, I observed their body language. I decided to confront Ethel about her sunglasses, but Anthony intervened, insisting he would bring them down from my bedroom. Determined, I spoke up.

"No, Ethel can come in with me to get them." I wanted to confront her about sleeping with my husband. Before I could, Anthony stormed in. Ethel's slight smile and her "oh no" response confirmed my suspicions. Angry, I ran upstairs and grabbed the sunglasses, crushing them in my hands. Anthony pinned me to the floor, punching my head. I broke free and ran outside where Ethel was with Angelina.

"Are you sleeping with my husband?" I demanded again.

She only smiled.

Anthony, behind me, ordered Ethel to take my keys. In a desperate act, I threw them into the woods, but they quickly found them. I locked myself inside the house, refusing to talk to Anthony. He left with Ethel and Angelina, taking my car keys. Late that night, Anthony returned, calling me crazy and claiming he didn't want our daughter around me alone anymore. From then on, he controlled when and how long I could see Angelina. Feeling manipulated and isolated, I questioned my sanity but knew I had to break free from his control.

The following day at work, I reached my breaking point. Constantly contacted by different girls—Natasha, Elena, Sofia, and now Ethel—I couldn't take it anymore. I called my parents, pleading for help to escape this life. I couldn't leave on my own; my paycheck went to mortgages and car payments, leaving me with nothing. Anthony controlled my finances, holding my debit and credit cards. My head was spinning, but I knew something had to change for Angelina and me. It was time to reclaim my life from Anthony's control.

···Chapter Eight

Admitting to myself that I had married a wolf in sheep's clothing was a harrowing realization. Looking back, I see that this was the point where the veil began to lift, revealing the true nature of Anthony. It wasn't entirely clear yet, but the picture was starting to change. The thought of telling my parents, family, and friends the full truth about my relationship with Anthony was agonizing. It took a monumental amount of courage to pick up the phone and call my dad. My parents had always welcomed me with open arms in times of need, and this time was no different.

One evening at work, I finally made the call. My voice trembled as I explained my situation. My dad, ever supportive, gave me the name and number of a lawyer. Morgan, my steadfast friend, offered me a place to stay for a few nights. With a mix of fear and resolve, I called the lawyer my dad had recommended, and we began the process. I left the car I had been driving at the farmhouse and spent the night at Morgan's house, seeking refuge from the storm that was my life.

That evening, I ignored Anthony's texts and calls. The silence must have unnerved him, as he sensed his grip on me was slipping. The next day, Morgan picked me up from work. As we drove away from the hospital, we saw Anthony's truck parked across the street in a gas station parking lot. He was watching, trying to keep track of my every move.

Morgan took back country roads to her house, a secluded route that felt like a lifeline. Anthony knew where she lived, but he didn't dare follow us. Morgan wouldn't hesitate to call the police, and Anthony knew that. Despite his attempts to intimidate me through Ethel's husband's nasty messages, I saw through the setup. The barrage of texts and calls continued, but I was determined to break free.

The following morning, Morgan and I went to work together. That afternoon, Anthony showed up at the hospital. He was cunning enough not to come to my unit, instead speaking to someone at the admissions desk and asking for Angelina's health insurance card. He claimed she was hurt and needed it. I knew better. Everything was on record at the hospital and her pediatrician's office. If she were truly hurt, she would be in the emergency department or admitted.

My manager, aware of the situation, called the police. This was the first time in eleven years that I had spoken to the police about my husband. Fear had always kept me from calling before; Anthony would take my phone and keys, leaving me powerless. He had brainwashed me into believing the police were bad people. But this day marked a turning point. The police took my report, and for the first time, I began to reclaim my power.

My mom picked me up from work, and we went shopping for essentials since I had none of my belongings. The next day, we visited the lawyer's office. My mind was still foggy, but I could see the truth of what Anthony had done to me over the years. The plan was to file for divorce and custody, a daunting task given my lack of knowledge about the legal system.

For the past decade, I had been micromanaged ... every minute of every day. The lawyer, Devra, was kind but direct. As I recounted my story, her reactions told me everything I needed to know. I was in an unhealthy, abusive relationship. Her empathy and professionalism made me realize the necessity of change.

Devra moved quickly, targeting the properties, finances, and custody issues all at once. It was overwhelming. Anthony had a power of attorney over me, a tool he used to sign over properties and deeds without my presence. I hadn't realized the extent of his control. He drained my bank account, but most of it had gone to bills anyway. He transferred our properties into a corporation with his business partner, Martin, moving faster than we could keep up.

I went to the courthouse to file for a Protection from Abuse (PFA) order. Telling my story to the woman there, including the times Anthony had beaten and handcuffed me, was both terrifying and liberating. Her reactions confirmed the severity of my situation. A few days later, Devra called, urging me to come to the courthouse immediately. My mom and I waited in a conference room, anxiety gnawing at us. When Devra arrived, she informed us that they had located Angelina. We needed to pick her up right away.

Angelina was at the farmhouse with Ethel. We drove there, police cars with flashing lights surrounding the property. Ethel stood on the porch, holding Angelina. As my mom and I approached, Ethel, looking terrified, had no choice but to hand Angelina over to me. Anthony was nowhere in sight. We quickly put Angelina in the car seat and drove to my parents' house.

Fearing for our safety, my parents arranged for Angelina and me to stay with my cousin, a police officer. For the next week, we hid out there while Devra worked on the custody hearing. Angelina enjoyed her time with my cousin's granddaughter, playing and riding horses in the serene, green fields. The picturesque setting, with horses grazing and mountains in the distance, was a stark contrast to the chaos of my life. It was the perfect place to find a moment of peace and gather strength for the battles ahead.

During all these major changes, Angelina never asked about her dad. At just two years old, her understanding of the tumultuous shifts in our lives was limited. She had been passed from one babysitter to another and had slept in too many different places for her young age. The instability in her early years weighed heavily on my heart. All I wanted was for her to be with me, to provide her with the stable upbringing she deserved. Despite everything, she kept her infectious smile and boundless happiness, a beacon of hope in my darkest moments.

While staying at my cousin's house, I had my phone and laptop with me. In hindsight, I wished I could have discarded them, severing all ties with social media and the toxic world it connected me to. One day, I logged onto Facebook and saw that Anthony had reactivated his account. He posted pictures of me, captioning them with claims of me being his "beautiful wife." He uploaded a photo of a house we had once planned to buy, featuring a German Shepherd puppy and a new car with a sign that read, "Welcome home Becky." The posts painted a false picture of a perfect life.

Anthony's deceit ran deeper. His girlfriends, the ones he had cheated on me with, bombarded me with messages on Skype, claiming that Anthony was serious about us and wanted to build a future together. His manipulation extended to his sister, a well-educated registered nurse. She called me, insisting that we needed to work through our problems and become a family. Our conversation lasted over an hour, and her words made me question everything. She was married to a pastor, and their seemingly perfect, religious family made me wonder if reconciliation was possible for us too.

It had only been two weeks since I had left Anthony, but the combined pressure from his sister and the deceptive Facebook posts created a whirlwind of emotions. I felt a frantic urgency to return to him. I called him, and he agreed to take me back. I even made a list of things I wanted to address in our relationship, naively believing that we could work through them. Anthony agreed to everything. He arranged for a friend to pick us up.

My cousin's family was out when Anthony's friend arrived. As we packed our belongings into the car, my cousin's wife and granddaughter returned home. They were crying, knowing the decision I was making was disastrous. I failed to see it then, but I was letting down my entire family. Returning to an abuser is a tragically common pattern, much like released prisoners finding themselves back behind bars. Despite the misery, the familiarity of the prison walls becomes a twisted form of comfort. Anthony was my prison. I went back because I clung to the hope that he would change, that I could help him. I loved him deeply and felt an overwhelming sense of responsibility to fix our relationship. My kindhearted, giving, and empathetic nature trapped me in a cycle of abuse. Anthony's sorrowful pleas for forgiveness and his promises blinded me to his severe emotional and psychological issues. I wasn't equipped to help him, but at that time, I didn't realize it. In going back, I enabled him, perpetuating the problem.

His friend drove us to Anthony's mom's house in Lancaster. Angelina and I unpacked our belongings yet again. Anthony's mom was cold and distant, but I was too emotionally drained to fully grasp it. She made us sleep on the cold, hard floor, giving us only a few blankets and small throw pillows from the couch. We shivered through the nights, and I woke up sore and stiff each morning. The stress and anxiety left me unable to eat; I subsisted on coffee and crackers. Anthony's mom didn't offer to take us grocery shopping, instead telling us to scavenge through her nearly empty pantry. My weight plummeted back down to one hundred pounds. I looked sick, and I felt even worse—both mentally and physically. We endured this for about a month, a month that felt like an eternity.

I hadn't seen Anthony since the day I filed a Protection from Abuse (PFA) order against him. Now, court was the only way to confront the man who had once been my world. In a cruel twist, he had Ethel file a PFA against me, and to make matters worse, he wrote out her complaint, fabricating a story that implied I was romantically involved with her. It was a tangled web of lies and manipulation.

April rolled around, marking Angelina's third birthday. Despite my best efforts, I had no money to give her the celebration she deserved. Anthony's mother, in a rare act of kindness, picked up a small pack of cupcakes from the grocery store. I tried to make the day special for Angelina. We went for a walk in the afternoon, each step weighed down by my guilt for not being able to do more, yet lightened by the simple joy of being together. Her laughter was a bittersweet reminder of the innocence I was fighting to protect.

The day of the court hearing arrived. I drove myself to the courthouse, my heart heavy with anxiety. The hallway outside the courtroom was packed with people, the air thick with cigarette smoke and the sound of swearing. I felt out of place, a lone soul dressed in my best attempt at court-appropriate attire, standing amidst chaos. I was unsure of where to sit, given Ethel's PFA against me. Just before we were called in, Anthony stepped off the elevator, looking tired and worn. Our eyes met, and I saw him suppress a smile before quickly looking away. Ethel arrived shortly after, avoiding my gaze entirely.

Inside the courtroom, I was called up first. I took an oath, and Ethel joined me to agree to drop her PFA. Then it was Anthony's turn. He stood next to me, and I agreed to drop my PFA against him. The judge dismissed us, and we walked out. Ethel left without a word, but Anthony lingered, following me to the parking garage. As soon as we got into the car, he kissed me, whispering that he loved and missed me. We returned to the farmhouse, where he was unusually kind, having gotten what he wanted. Later that day, he brought a black BMW SUV to the house, claiming it was now mine. But his generosity was a facade; he revealed that everything, including the houses, insurance, and cars, were no longer in my name.

Ethel visited later that week, and I apologized to her. She accepted, but the trust was shattered. Anthony confessed that he had gotten drunk while I was away but insisted he didn't sleep with Ethel, a confession that left me questioning his intentions. He claimed he could have slept with her if he wanted to, but he didn't. Naively, I believed him.

May marked our seven-year anniversary. Anthony had never been one for grand gestures, but this year, he told me to dress up for a special night. He arrived with a bouquet of flowers and took me to dinner at the Hotel Hershey. We sat outside, taking pictures—something Anthony rarely did unless he was drunk. For one night, we were a couple without conflict, sharing a fleeting moment of peace. But the illusion shattered quickly. Anthony blamed me for our financial troubles, saying my attempt to divorce him cost us the house he had flaunted on Facebook. He convinced me to take out a mortgage on the farmhouse to pay off the Mercedes and make repairs, promising it would bring us closer. I believed him and took out the mortgage in my name. The money vanished almost immediately.

Within a week, the arguments resumed. One afternoon, as we argued in the living room about his broken promises, his frustration boiled over. He grabbed my head and slapped me hard across the face. I bolted for the door, knowing what would come next. He chased me outside, screaming threats. When I refused to go back inside, he knocked me to the ground and dragged me by my hair behind the car, away from prying eyes. I tried to scream, but he covered my mouth, his grip tightening. He hauled me back into the house, demanding sex. When I refused, he slapped me again and ordered me to shower. The hot water stung my scraped skin, blood mingling with the dirt and gravel embedded in my wounds. I sat in the tub, sobbing, praying for an end to the nightmare. I complied with his demands, broken and defeated.

Amid this turmoil, my dog Pinch fell ill. His neck swelled, his weight dropped, and tumors appeared on his chest. Despite my pleas, Anthony refused to take him to the vet, dismissing Pinch's suffering. As a narcissist, Anthony only cared for animals that served a purpose, and a sick dog was of no use to him. Pinch's condition worsened, and I did my best to keep him clean and comfortable. One Sunday, he fell unconscious. I sat with him, soothing him as he moaned and barked, telling him it was okay to let go. Anthony showed no compassion, insisting we go out to dinner, leaving Pinch alone in his final moments.

When we returned, the house was eerily silent. I found Pinch had passed away. I called Anthony, who came with a garbage bag and gloves, treating Pinch's body with callous disregard. He threw my beloved dog into a trash can, ignoring my pleas for a proper burial. The next day, Pinch was gone. Anthony claimed he buried him in the backyard, but there were no signs of disturbed earth. He had lied, discarding Pinch like trash. The cruelty and heartlessness of Anthony's actions left a scar that would never heal.

The following summer, during the days that I had off from work Anthony allowed Angelina to stay with me alone. It was a good summer for Angelina and I. She loved to visit the library. It was a smaller library near train tracks. She enjoyed watching the trains go by. Inside the library they had a train table, and she played with the trains with the other kids. She picked out her books and we took them home and read almost all of them before bedtime. At the end of the summer the library had a celebration for all the kids who read books. This was a fun carnival at one of the parks nearby. Angelina and I were allowed to go per Anthony by ourselves. She had a great time.

Angelina and I spent most of our days at the park down the road from the farmhouse. She loved to run around on the playground and ride her big wheel bike down the trails. We took a trip to Hershey Park, but Ethel had to go with us. Angelina and I still had a great time riding the train and other little kid rides. When we were home together Angelina helped me cook dinner and for a treat, we ate ice cream if Anthony bought it for us. We had a baby pool that we spent the hot days playing in. We picked blackberries and made jelly together. She was a big help in the kitchen and always wanted to learn. With what little we did have we made the best of it.

Anthony wanted me to become closer friends with Ethel since she didn't have many friends. The friends that she did have did not want to be around her because they didn't like Anthony. Ethel and I continued to go shopping and hang out together. Anthony even allowed us to hang out at a bar that he was a silent partner within Harrisburg. He allowed me to drink and go out but only with Ethel. I was sometimes allowed to hang out with a friend of mine from work and go to the bars with them. I felt like I had some freedom.

Anthony still would not stay overnight with me at the farmhouse. He started to tell me again that I needed to come back to the house after drinking with Ethel and if we all slept together, he would start staying overnight and not leave me. His promises and threats were happening again. The only times he stayed overnight was when Ethel was there. He was back to his old self again. He never kept his promises.

On August 13th, 2015, I made one of the biggest mistakes of my life. I signed over full custody of Angelina to Anthony. He came to the house and told me, "I'm in trouble with the IRS." He did a lot of shady stuff, so it was believable. Anthony's eyes were tearing, and he was very serious. For the safety of, and fear for Angelina I agreed to what Anthony wanted me to do. I knew nothing about changing custody orders. I should have received papers from the court stating that Anthony had a complaint and wanted to modify our custody order. I never received anything. It was documented that I was served papers for this, but I was never served. Ethel was the one who was served the papers.

Anthony and Ethel worked together to get me to sign all my custody over. He stopped by the farmhouse on my day off and we went to the courthouse. He made it sound like this was a small thing that we were doing. He promised that we would reverse the order in two months after he wasn't in trouble anymore. He said, "I might be going into a witness protection program at some point but don't worry about it."

The way he made it sound I feared for Angelina, and I agreed. I signed the papers that agreed that Anthony could move to Hungary with Angelina, and I had no custody. It was all very crazy at the time, but I did it because I loved and trusted Anthony. I was terrified for Angelina's safety. He wrote the custody agreement up that they would move to Hungary. I knew this was too bizarre to believe that they would move to Hungary.

This whole time that Ethel was with him I didn't know they had a secret apartment in the city. I found out from Ethel's ex-boyfriend that she had been dating and living with Anthony since the winter of 2014. This was when I first met her on my birthday. Ethel was a very good liar. She convinced me that she got a job at a clothing store and no longer worked for Anthony. She had me believing that she disliked Anthony and only wanted to be friends with me. She even said that her aunt that lives in Harrisburg has been watching Angelina since she started her new job.

When Anthony made me sleep with her, she never protested. She tried to act like sometimes she only wanted to be with me but looking back now I can see that Anthony was training her to like girls just the same as he trained me. Anthony was back to his sick mind games.

Anthony loved to control everyone and everything. He convinced me that he had cameras set up everywhere in the house and in my car. He said to me, "I can hear what you're talking about all the time. I'm watching you all the time. I even have your phone tapped." I was terrified of him, so I believed him. By believing everything he was telling me made me feel like I never had my own privacy and I had to listen or do everything he told me to, or I had to face the consequences. I was traumatized emotionally by this added stress.

Anthony kept encouraging me to go out to bars with Ethel and to get drunk and come back to the farmhouse. I played his game because he made me believe that this was normal.

A close friend from work Nina, invited me out to celebrate her birthday. Ethel came with me because Anthony told me that she had to. Nina had invited a few of her friends also. We were planning on going to dinner and then to a bar down the street. It was a nice warm evening and we all sat outside on the restaurant patio under bright yellow umbrellas overlooking the square of Hershey talking and laughing. The patio had beautiful purple and pink flowers in large planters. You could look out across the street and see the Hershey kiss streetlights and hear people screaming that were riding the rollercoasters in Hershey Park. Families were walking up and down the sidewalks and going to the ice cream shop down the street. We were dressed up nicely wearing pretty dresses. Our appetizers and entrees came out and were delicious. It was nice to be able to order what I wanted. We had a slice of chocolate cake with a candle lit in it brought out to Nina while we sang happy birthday to her. Next, we drove down the street to a gas station that was turned into a bar. Entering the bar, the music was loud, and we all took shots at the bar. It was packed and people were dancing and having a good time. Ethel wouldn't get in any of the pictures with us which I felt was odd instead she offered to take all the pictures. We drank a lot and danced too. We were all having so much fun that I almost felt careless and free for a moment. Soon Anthony started texting me to hurry up and get back to the farmhouse. The fun was over because I had to listen to Anthony. We left and arrived at the farmhouse where Anthony got what he wanted. I did everything he wanted me to do, and he never held up his end of deal of living and sleeping with me every night.

The following summer, during the precious days I had off from work, Anthony allowed Angelina to stay with me alone. It felt like a small victory, a sliver of normalcy in the chaos that had become my life. That summer became a haven for Angelina and me. We found joy in the simplest of things, like our regular visits to the quaint library near the train tracks. Angelina adored watching the trains thunder by, her eyes wide with wonder. Inside, she spent hours at the train table, her laughter blending with the chatter of other children. She carefully selected her books, and we read almost all of them before bedtime, her little voice echoing the words as we snuggled close.

As summer drew to a close, the library hosted a celebration for the children who had participated in the reading program. It was a vibrant carnival at a nearby park, and for once, Anthony permitted us to go alone.

Angelina's excitement was infectious as she ran from game to game, her face painted with delight. It was one of those rare, perfect days that felt like a bubble of happiness in a turbulent sea. Most days, we found ourselves at the park down the road from the farmhouse. Angelina would race around the playground, her laughter ringing out like a melody. She loved riding her big wheel bike down the trails, her cheeks flushed with joy.

On one special outing, we ventured to Hershey Park. Although Ethel had to accompany us, Angelina and I still cherished the day, riding the train and enjoying the little kid rides. Back at home, Angelina loved to help me cook dinner, and as a treat, we would savor ice cream if Anthony had bought some. On hot days, we splashed in a baby pool, our laughter mingling with the summer breeze. We picked blackberries and made jelly, her small hands eager to help in the kitchen. Despite having so little, we created a world of joy and learning together.

Anthony had a twisted idea of fostering a friendship between Ethel and me, likely to exert more control. Ethel lacked friends because no one wanted to be around her due to their disdain for Anthony. Despite my reservations, we shopped and hung out together, even visiting a bar where Anthony was a silent partner. He allowed me to drink and go out, but only with Ethel. Occasionally, I could meet a friend from work and visit bars, a semblance of freedom that felt almost foreign.

Yet, Anthony never stayed overnight at the farmhouse, unless Ethel was there. He dangled promises and threats, saying if we all slept together, he would start staying with me. It was a cruel game, one he never intended to keep. His manipulations resumed, and one August day, I made a grievous mistake. Anthony arrived, visibly distressed, claiming he was in trouble with the IRS. His eyes glistened with tears, and his serious demeanor sparked fear for Angelina's safety. Desperate and afraid, I agreed to his demands. I signed over full custody of Angelina, believing his promises that it was temporary, a necessary measure for her safety. He spun tales of witness protection and danger, and in my terror, I complied.

Unbeknownst to me, Ethel and Anthony had a secret apartment in the city. Ethel's ex-boyfriend revealed their deceit, that she had been living with Anthony since the previous winter, the very time I first met her. Ethel was a masterful liar, convincing me she had a new job and despised Anthony. She claimed her aunt was watching Angelina, but it was all a ruse. When Anthony coerced me into sleeping with her, she never resisted, pretending to desire me. In hindsight, I see now that Anthony was grooming her, just as he had groomed me, playing his sick mind games. Anthony thrived on control. He convinced me that he had cameras everywhere, even in my car, and that my phone was tapped. He claimed to hear everything, watching my every move. His psychological manipulation left me feeling constantly monitored, stripping away any sense of privacy or autonomy. The emotional trauma was overwhelming.

He encouraged me to go out with Ethel, to drink and return to the farmhouse. I played along, believing this facade of normalcy. One evening, a close friend from work, Nina, invited me out for her birthday. Ethel came along, as Anthony insisted. We planned a dinner followed by a bar visit. The evening was perfect; we sat on a restaurant patio under bright yellow umbrellas, overlooking the square of Hershey. The air was filled with the scent of flowers from large planters, and the distant sounds of rollercoasters and families added to the festive atmosphere. We laughed, talked, and enjoyed delicious food. A slice of chocolate cake with a candle for Nina capped the dinner.

We moved to a bar, formerly a gas station, where the music was loud and the energy high. We took shots, danced, and for a fleeting moment, I felt carefree. Ethel, however, stayed out of the pictures, a quiet observer. The night was magical until Anthony's texts started, demanding my return to the farmhouse. The spell was broken. We left, and upon arrival, Anthony got what he wanted, as always. His promises of living and sleeping with me every night remained unfulfilled, a cruel reminder of his unending control.

The following day, Anthony's call came like a thunderstorm, his voice crackling with rage. He started yelling at me, accusing me of dancing with other guys at the bar the night before. The accusation was as false as it was hurtful—I had only danced with my friends. But Anthony's fury was relentless.

"I know the bar owner," he screamed. "I can get his video surveillance of you dancing with random guys!" His words stung, each one a painful lash, accusing me of infidelity. I tried to defend myself, insisting I hadn't danced with anyone else, but my protests fell on deaf ears. Anthony was adamant, claiming Ethel had seen me dancing with other guys all night, twisting the knife deeper into my heart.

A few nights later, Ethel and I found ourselves sitting outside a Starbucks, sipping coffee. I was venting my frustrations about how Anthony wasn't bringing Angelina around as much as he used to. Ethel's response was startling.

"Why are you with him? Why don't you just leave him and marry someone else?"

Her words hung in the air, heavy with implications. It was odd coming from her, as she had never suggested I leave Anthony. She knew we were supposedly working on fixing our marriage, yet here she was, planting seeds of doubt.

That fall, my life spiraled into a grueling routine. I took on extra shifts at the hospital, working my standard twelve-hour days and adding another four hours, turning them into sixteen-hour marathons. On my days off, I picked up night shifts to help with the understaffed unit. The constant switch between day and night shifts exhausted me, leaving my body and mind in a state of perpetual fatigue. Anxiety gnawed at me, fueled by the ever-widening chasm between me and my daughter.

Desperate for relief, I went to the doctor and asked for something to help with my anxiety and sleep. A friend at work had found solace in medication, so I thought I'd try it too, even though I knew I was sensitive to such treatments. The doctor prescribed Ativan, starting me on the lowest dose. I knew the risks—it was easily addictive—but I needed something.

On the days I didn't work, I took the medication, and it helped me relax and sleep. For the first time in a long while, I felt a semblance of calm.

Anthony, ever the manipulator, wanted me to invite Ethel over and get drunk with her. Dutifully, I complied. As we sat on the porch, drinking and talking, I opened up about my past hurts. I told her about the other girls who had been involved with Anthony, each thinking they would be the one he'd leave me for. I showed her messages and pictures, my voice trembling with the pain of betrayal. Sofia, one of the girls, still texted me, urging me to leave Anthony alone.

Ethel and Sofia had met a few times, and later Sofia revealed that Anthony wanted her to move into a cabin up north so Ethel could live with him in the city apartment, while I would stay at the farmhouse. It was a ludicrous plan. I had only met Sofia once, but Ethel worked with her. Ethel dismissed Sofia as dumb, saying her job was to wash Anthony's cars, implying he was using her for free labor. But in truth, we were all workers in Anthony's twisted game, used for labor and sex. Human trafficking thrives on force, fraud, or coercion to compel someone into work or commercial sex acts. Reflecting on my situation, I wondered if we were all victims of human trafficking. Anthony used a variety of control tactics—physical and emotional abuse, threats, isolation, and economic manipulation. I felt trapped, only ever paid once when I first met him at his restaurant.

After a few drinks, Anthony arrived, adding to the tension. He expected me to serve him dinner and drinks while he lounged on the couch, watching a movie. He found my bottle of Ativan, opened it, and forced pills into my mouth, claiming we were going to have fun. We continued drinking, and I became very drunk. Anthony led us upstairs, where he started kissing both Ethel and me. My vision blurred, my body felt like lead, and the last thing I saw was the bed before I blacked out completely. I woke up the next morning, disoriented, with Ethel lying next to me. Mixing Ativan with alcohol was dangerous, and I had no idea how many pills Anthony had made me take. I could have died. My body felt paralyzed, my eyes open but unable to move. Anthony entered the room and had sex with me, then turned to Ethel and did the same. I felt dazed, drugged, unable to resist or comprehend fully what was happening.

When Anthony left, Ethel seemed unaffected, while I felt a bone-deep exhaustion. I wondered if he had given me something more than Ativan. I slept for most of the day, my body unable to muster any strength. I felt like I had a severe cold or virus, taking Nyquil to try and ease my symptoms. The next morning, I forced myself to work, despite still feeling sick.

At work, my clinical head nurse noticed my dilated pupils and reported me to the manager. Despite my ability to perform my job safely, I was called into the office with HR and a union representative. Terrified, I called Anthony, who told me to cooperate. HR drove me to a third-party location for a urine drug test. I explained about the Ativan and Nyquil, but the outcome was uncertain. Anthony had the prescription bottle, and my job depended on whether he would provide it. Anthony, holding my fate in his hands, eventually sent a picture of the pill bottle. I forwarded it to the doctor, and after a week, the lab results confirmed my story. I was cleared to return to work, but the experience left me shaken and humiliated. I spoke to a nurse friend and applied for a position in radiology, hoping for a fresh start.

Returning to my unit was awkward and embarrassing, but my coworkers were supportive, knowing about my home life. Some shared similar experiences, making me feel less alone. Still, the fear of losing my career was a constant shadow. A few weeks later, I transferred to radiology, a smaller, more welcoming unit. The work was easier, a relief from the relentless trauma patients. Despite everything, I tried to carry on, finding solace in the new environment and the support of my new colleagues.

Thanksgiving was approaching, and the air was thick with the chill of uncertainty. I asked Anthony what our plans were, but his response was elusive, leaving a void where clarity should have been. Since the day I left my cousin's house, I hadn't spoken to my parents. Our family ties were frayed, nearly severed by my actions, and the thought of the holidays without them was a deep, aching wound. I missed the warmth and chaos of family gatherings, the laughter, the shared meals. Anthony's mom had become a distant figure, her calls dwindling to once a month, and our visits to Lancaster ceased altogether since moving to the farmhouse. Without any clear direction from Anthony, I assumed we would spend Thanksgiving with his family.

On Thanksgiving Day, my anxiety mounted as I repeatedly tried to call and text Anthony, desperate to know our plans. Late that morning, he arrived at the farmhouse with Angelina, dressed adorably in a little dress.

"Just get in the truck, we're going to eat," he snapped.

Confused, I complied, wondering why they were dressed up if we were just heading to a Chinese buffet. The day felt hollow, and I was acutely aware of how much I missed Angelina. Seeing her so infrequently was torture, a slow, relentless ache. At the buffet, I tried to savor every moment with Angelina, despite the palpable annoyance radiating from Anthony. I was walking on eggshells, terrified of saying anything that might anger him and jeopardize my time with my daughter. I harbored a fleeting hope that we might spend the rest of the day together or visit his family, but it was clear that I was not part of his holiday plans. After the meal, he drove me back to the farmhouse.

"Goodbye, Rebecca," Angelina said before they drove off.

The words cut deeper than any knife. She had started calling me by my name instead of "mom," a change Anthony seemed to encourage. It was a small but devastating shift, a sign of my diminishing presence in her life.

Anthony's indifference was a stark reminder that he was moving on, building a new life without me. He claimed to love me and still slept with me, but it was clear that I was merely a financial asset, funding his lifestyle with his new victim, Ethel. When Ethel visited, she spoke little of Anthony, instead talking about reconciling with her husband, who worked in North Carolina. Her casual demeanor suggested she had moved on, but

I knew better. Anthony was weaving his web around her, just as he had done with me.

Christmas brought another painful episode. Anthony waited until late afternoon to bring Angelina to me, claiming they had been at the restaurant, a lie I saw through. When he finally arrived, he kept a tight grip on Angelina, dictating what she should eat and play with, maintaining his control. Every move I made was under his watchful eye, his presence a constant reminder of the power he held. Angelina's occasional use of another language and her comment, "Rebecca doesn't understand," were heartbreaking. She had grown accustomed to leaving me and calling me by my name, signs of Anthony's manipulation.

One day, while taking Angelina out to eat with Ethel, she accidentally called Ethel "mommy." The word stung like a bee. When I questioned Ethel, she dismissed it as a child's imagination, but my heart knew better. Angelina often talked about a purple room, a detail Anthony and Ethel brushed off as fantasy. But I suspected there was more to it, a hidden life I was not privy to.

That year, Anthony's deceit reached a new level. He tricked me into signing divorce papers without my knowledge. Court documents were intercepted, and Ethel accepted them in my absence. One day, Anthony took me to his friend's auto garage, claiming I needed to sign property-related papers. His friend's wife, a notary, guided me through the signatures without explanation. Anthony flipped through the pages, and I trusted him, unaware that I was signing away my marriage. It wasn't until later that I discovered the truth—I was officially divorced without my consent.

Anthony had orchestrated everything, weaving his lies and manipulations to strip me of my family, my daughter, and my sense of self. The holidays, once a time of joy and togetherness, had become a stark reminder of my isolation and loss.

··· Chapter Nine

I woke up shivering in my bed, the cold farmhouse pressing in on me like an unwelcome embrace. The silence was deafening. There were no warm sounds of Angelina's laughter, no dogs barking, no horses galloping through the fields. It was just me and the oppressive quiet. I sat up slowly, rubbing my eyes, and tried to rise, but my bones ached and cracked—a prelude to arthritis that I didn't know was beginning to take hold. I walked towards the bathroom, glancing out the window to see a grey, dreary morning with frost covering the ground like a thin, icy blanket. Turning to the mirror, I barely recognized the reflection staring back at me: hollow eyes with dark bags beneath them, a face that looked sick and sunken.

Who was this person?

It was my thirtieth birthday.

As I stood there, I couldn't help but think of my friends who had turned thirty, celebrating with grand vacations and big parties. *What did I have to look forward to?* Anthony had promised to take me out to dinner. It wasn't much, but it was better than spending the day alone. When he picked me up from the farmhouse, he didn't bring Angelina. He still refused to stay the night at the farmhouse, despite his promises. I took a deep breath, telling myself that dinner was better than nothing.

Anthony had chosen a Mexican restaurant, knowing it was my favorite cuisine. The meal was pleasant, and for a brief moment, we got along. I dared to hope that maybe, just maybe, we could be the perfect family I dreamed of. I wanted to capture the moment, to take a picture of us together, clinging to the belief that we could still be a loving family. Anthony, always the manipulator, allowed it, repeating his mantra that if I just did what he said, we would live together happily.

After dinner, Anthony spoke of big plans. He mentioned that someone might buy his restaurant. This news filled me with a glimmer of hope—perhaps he would finally come home to the farmhouse. When I asked, he confirmed it with a smile, adding that we would start looking for a house soon. We went shopping, and he even let me pick out clothes, a rare indulgence. But then he bought several suitcases, explaining that they were for keeping Angelina's belongings organized when they went to the cabin. It struck me as odd, but I didn't question it further. At the time, Anthony was having me take out credit cards to pay off other credit cards. We were drowning in debt, making minimum payments on twelve cards. Anthony dismissed my concerns, promising that selling the restaurant or cabin would resolve our financial woes.

Our weekends often involved trips to flea markets and antique shops. In the spring, we visited a flea market where Anthony bought more old suitcases. His explanation remained the same—organizing belongings at the restaurant or cabin. By summer, Anthony was still bringing Angelina to see me once a week, but he pushed me to pick up extra shifts at the hospital, claiming we needed the money. This left me with little time for Angelina, and my heart shattered with each excuse he gave for not bringing her. Sometimes weeks would pass without seeing her. I was isolated, cut off from my family and friends, utterly alone.

Ethel continued to visit the farmhouse, insisting she wanted nothing to do with Anthony. She claimed she only wanted to be friends, expressing discomfort with Anthony's attempts to involve her in his sexual fantasies. Ethel and I spent some time together at the pool, but Anthony forbade bringing Angelina. Our interactions were increasingly confined to public places, under Anthony's watchful eye. I began to see how Anthony used Angelina as a pawn to control me. Parental alienation was his weapon, turning my daughter against me. I was riddled with anxiety, anger, and fear, watching helplessly as Angelina became estranged due to Anthony's psychological manipulation. He constantly accused me of infidelity, monitoring my every move, and attacking me if I didn't respond quickly enough. My frustration grew, and I found myself arguing more with Anthony, a dangerous game.

One evening, Ethel's lies about me pushed Anthony over the edge. He stormed into the farmhouse, yelling accusations. I yelled back, my anger boiling over. In a terrifying moment, he grabbed a kitchen knife and held it to my throat. I wasn't scared—I knew he wouldn't kill me—but the threat was real. He shoved me to the floor and kicked me in the stomach, knocking the wind out of me. His new tactic was spitting on me, a degrading act that left me feeling utterly humiliated. He blamed me for his violence, claiming his hands hurt from hitting me so often.

Anthony's manipulation extended to my family. He convinced me they didn't love me, wouldn't help me if I left. I knew it wasn't true, but I believed him anyway. That summer, I sank into depression, longing for the family I wanted but never had. I dreamed of more children, of a home filled with love, but Anthony's promises were empty. We spent my rare days off doing physical labor, salvaging construction supplies from a nearby property, all for a future that would never come.

When our passports arrived, Anthony took them immediately, promising a family vacation to Italy. I didn't even get to hold my passport. It was another lie, another way to control me.

The first of August was a day that started with so much promise. Anthony brought Angelina to the farmhouse, and my heart swelled with joy. Earlier that summer, Angelina and I had planted a row of sunflowers by the picket fence, and now they stood tall and proud, their yellow heads turned towards the sun. I had her stand in front of them, the vibrant flowers forming a natural backdrop. She grinned, her big, toothy smile lighting up her face as she yelled, "cheese!" She wore her favorite pink sweatshirt jacket and a pink heart shirt, radiating innocence and happiness. She ran back to me, and we took a few more pictures together, her tiny arms wrapped around my neck as we smiled for the camera.

We cooked burgers on the grill and had a cozy dinner, just the two of us. It was a small but precious moment, a rare time when we could connect as mother and daughter. Little did I know, this would be the last time I would see her. The picture we took that day has since become a source of immense pain, a haunting reminder of a time that slipped through my fingers.

I had always dreamed of a family vacation to the beach, but Anthony always had excuses—he was too busy, or he had to work. His refrain was always the same.

"If you want to live a good life and not have to work all the time, we have to work hard now."

That summer, I received a bonus and pleaded with him to go to the beach, even if just for a weekend. To my surprise, he agreed, and I was elated. Finally, a mini family vacation seemed within reach.

Towards the end of July, Ethel had texted me, saying she was moving back in with her ex-husband in North Carolina, and they were planning to move to California together. It all happened so fast. She owed me a few hundred dollars but refused to pay me back. I decided to cut ties with her, telling Anthony about it. Oddly, he wasn't concerned, which was uncharacteristic for him. Anthony always made sure to get his money back. That was the last I heard from Ethel, and I thought she was out of my life for good.

Anthony was supposed to be at the farmhouse with Angelina so we could go to the beach in Delaware for a long weekend, the same beach where we used to keep our boat. He arrived around noon, but to my dismay, he was alone. My heart sank.

"Where is Angelina? This is supposed to be our little vacation."

"I wanted to have a romantic weekend, just us."

He hadn't mentioned this until we were about to leave, and I had packed everything for Angelina. He explained that she was staying at his mom's house. Though I was crushed, we had already paid for the hotel and had everything packed. I bit my lip and got into the truck, trying to hold back my tears. As soon as I sat down, he slapped me for arguing. He drove recklessly, tailgating and taking turns aggressively. He refused to use the air conditioning, making the ride unbearable. His mood was as hot and oppressive as the air around us.

We stopped at a liquor store before checking into the hotel. I was so sick from the heat and his erratic driving that I started vomiting as soon as we parked. Once in the hotel room, I took my migraine medication while he started drinking. When I began to feel better, we walked to a nearby bar. Anthony's demeanor changed like a light switch—he became flirty and nice, as if nothing had happened. He pointed out other girls at the bar, suggesting we invite one of them to our room. I was there to relax, not to cater to his fantasies. We returned to the hotel, and he continued drinking.

The next morning, we had breakfast and then headed to the beach. Anthony refused to wear sunscreen and got badly sunburned. He begrudgingly agreed to take one picture with me, warning me not to post it on social media. He was jealous and controlling, even making me delete bikini photos from my accounts. For the next few days, Anthony stayed in the hotel room, drinking because of his sunburn, while I spent my mornings alone on the beach. The ocean had always been a place of peace for me, a sanctuary where I could reflect on happier times. My childhood was filled with family vacations at the beach, and those memories stood in stark contrast to my present reality.

During our stay, Anthony confided that he might be in trouble, possibly facing jail or needing to go into witness protection with Angelina.

He said I couldn't join them because I needed to keep my job and maintain our properties. He insisted he was the reason I became a nurse, reminding me of the control he had over my life. I knew he was in trouble with the IRS and suspected he was involved in other shady dealings. His grandiose self-image made him believe he was untouchable.

Anthony often boasted about his legal troubles, claiming he always got off with just a fine because of his "really good lawyer." Whether his stories were true or not, I was forced to accept them as reality. Surprisingly, we didn't have any physical fights during our beach stay, but the tension was palpable. On the day we left, Anthony was anxious and spoke little. When I asked about seeing Angelina, he lied, saying it would be in a few days. We returned to the farmhouse, and he left after we unpacked.

A week passed without any sign of Anthony or Angelina. The night before Labor Day, Anthony called, repeating his story about witness protection and urging me to stay strong for our family. He said it would only be a few months. I insisted on being with them, but he refused, saying it was impossible. He even told me not to inform his mom. On Labor Day, one of Anthony's friends called, saying they had "scooped up" Anthony and Angelina. I broke down, not understanding what "scooped up" meant. *Was it the police?*

A few minutes later, his friend arrived at the farmhouse, expressing sympathy and surprise that I had lasted so long with Anthony. His words were confusing and alarming. He wouldn't tell me where they were, leaving me in a state of shock and confusion. He offered to help if I needed anything, but I felt utterly alone. I collapsed on the floor, crying uncontrollably.

Moments after he left, my phone started to ring, and it was Anthony's friend who was just at my house. I said hello and he started to ramble over me.

"Hey, how's Europe? I...?"

"Hello. This is Rebecca," I responded.

He quickly changed the subject and tried to cover up what he first said. He told me that he could help me find a puppy, so I wouldn't be so lonely, and it would help pass time. I knew in the back of my mind that something wasn't right.

Desperate, I called Nina, who knew my situation. She urged me to report Angelina missing to the police. I was hesitant, having given up custody months ago, but Nina insisted. It was time to take action, to fight for my daughter, even if it felt like a losing battle.

My mind couldn't comprehend the whirlwind of events unfolding around me, and I found myself paralyzed with indecision. I decided against calling the police, choosing instead to believe Anthony, who I had always trusted implicitly. Questioning him felt like a betrayal, and I feared that seeking help or sharing my fears with others would only result in losing any chance of seeing Angelina again.

I was trapped in a cycle of abuse, a prisoner of Battered Woman Syndrome, a condition that left me feeling responsible for all the stress and turmoil in Anthony's life. I hid the abuse from friends and family, fearing for Angelina's safety above all else. I did whatever Anthony thought was right for our family, even as my own health deteriorated under the immense stress. The symptoms of PTSD—flashbacks, dissociative states, and violent outbursts against the abuser—became part of my daily life. I suffered from chronic pain, high blood pressure, and depression, all while trying to maintain a facade of normalcy.

After hanging up with my friend, I called Anthony's mom, hoping for some clarity. Her reaction was bizarrely detached; instead of sharing my sense of urgency, she talked about her own medical and family problems. It felt as though she had been coached on how to respond if I called, displaying no concern for the gravity of the situation. Throughout that week, Anthony's mom called me nightly, but never mentioned Anthony or Angelina. I poured out my heart, explaining how seldom Anthony brought Angelina around and how it hurt me to my core. She seemed indifferent, quickly steering the conversation back to herself. It was as if my concerns for Angelina were inconsequential.

A week later, I received an email from Anthony. He claimed to be in a place where he had no control over his daily activities, hoping it would only be a few months before he and Angelina could return. His words offered little solace. A few months before Anthony left, he had taken our dog, Wolf, away without explanation. Despite my despair, I decided to search for a German Shepherd puppy, my favorite breed. I found a breeder nearby and put a deposit on a female puppy, the biggest of the litter, with black fur and tan legs. I named her Brigitte, and she became my lifeline, helping me endure the unbearable loneliness.

My friend from work visited with her kids to see the puppy and check on me. She urged me to call the police, but I clung to Anthony's promise that everything would return to normal in a few months. She saw through his lies, but my mind was too clouded by hope and fear to listen.

That November, I tried to call Anthony's mom again, but she didn't answer. Her silence was deafening. Desperate for information, I searched the internet and discovered that Anthony and Ethel had applied for a marriage license, confirming they were married the previous December. The realization hit me like a ton of bricks, and I began to vomit from the shock. The lie his friend had accidentally revealed—asking about Europe—suddenly made sense. Anthony and Ethel had likely moved to Europe together, and my rushed passport renewal now seemed like part of a larger plan.

Consumed by anger, depression, and a sense of betrayal, my thoughts spiraled. I felt utterly alone, with no one to turn to. Desperation led me to contemplate suicide. I watched a video on how to fashion a noose and found a thick rope in the barn. Climbing into the attic, I tied the rope around a beam, hot tears streaming down my face. Standing on a shaky wooden chair, I put the noose around my neck, ready to end my suffering. But then my phone beeped. I stepped back onto the chair, removed the noose, and collapsed on the floor. I couldn't go through with it, knowing that Angelina would have to live with the knowledge that her mother had taken her own life.

The message was from Anthony, threatening to call the police if I didn't respond. He claimed his marriage to Ethel was fake, part of a ruse to throw off those who were after him. He insisted it was all part of the plan and not to worry. Exhausted and emotionally shattered, I showered and cried myself to sleep, alone.

A week before Thanksgiving, feeling isolated and sad, I called my mom. She invited me to come home for Thanksgiving, but I declined. On Thanksgiving Day, I lay on the couch, watching television, my new routine of waking up, going to work, working out, playing with Brigitte, and then waiting for my family to return consuming my days. A loud knock at the door startled me. I saw Anthony's truck in the driveway and opened the door to find him looking rough, tired, and dirty. He didn't kiss me but sat on the couch, showing me a keychain with a red light, claiming it was how the witness protection people tracked him. He said it worked like a GPS, making the situation seem all the more believable.

He reminded me not to tell anyone about his situation, especially my coworkers. I confessed that I had told my friend and called his mom. He explained that his mom was upset with him for going into the program. Anthony then raided the fridge and my wallet, taking all the cash. He claimed the living conditions were horrible and that he missed me. He couldn't disclose their location, saying it would put him and Angelina in danger.

Anthony kissed me, reiterated his love and called me his wife. He reassured me that his marriage to Ethel was a lie and that he didn't know what had happened to her. He left, promising it wouldn't be much longer and urging me to stay strong for our family. As I watched him drive away, I felt a mixture of hope and despair. I clung to his words, desperate for a return to normalcy, yet deep down, I knew the truth was far more complicated and painful than I could bear to admit.

··· **Chapter Ten**

The days and nights stretched endlessly, each moment a torturous reminder of my isolation. Anthony wielded this isolation like a weapon, tightening his grip on my mind and soul. If I just went to work and did my job, it meant an easy paycheck for Anthony, allowing him to sustain his double life. I had already become adept at making excuses to avoid social gatherings with family, friends, and coworkers. Anthony had conditioned me to prioritize him above all else.

He continued his manipulation through emails and Skype messages, forbidding me from calling him or speaking to Angelina. His daily reminders to keep silent and his vague assurances that it would only be a few more months played on my fears. He painted a picture of himself trapped in a miserable existence among strangers, which only deepened my sympathy for him and my terror for Angelina.

Anthony was a classic narcissist, living multiple lives to feed his insatiable need for attention and admiration. He thrived on the thrill of meeting new people and ensnaring them in his web of lies. Foreign women intrigued by the idea of staying in America were his favorite targets, their fascination inflating his ego. He relished the control he had over them, and by extension, over me. No amount of my love or time could satisfy him because he was always seeking more. When I discovered his other lives, he would concoct new lies or blame me for his infidelities. Eventually, he disappeared with Angelina, entangling himself in yet another life, leaving me to face the consequences alone.

As Christmas approached, I clung to a desperate hope that they would be released in time for the holidays. I ordered board games, Barbie dolls, and crafts for Angelina, wrapping everything and filling her bedroom with presents. Meanwhile, practical concerns weighed on me. My car's tires were worn out, and I had no money for replacements. Anthony arranged for his friend, who owned a nearby garage, to install new tires. When I picked up the car, Martin, Anthony's friend, seemed unusually distant, avoiding eye contact, and not asking how I was doing. The next day, the car's battery died. Anthony sent his friends from the garage to fix it, but they were equally reticent, as if they were all in on a secret that I wasn't privy to.

One night, low on gas and out of money, I texted Anthony. He sent a friend to drop off cash, but this friend also avoided eye contact and didn't ask how I was. Recognizing this man as the one who had officiated Anthony's marriage to Ethel, I felt a chill of unease. It was as if everyone around me knew something I didn't.

On Christmas I sought solace at my parents' house, enjoying dinner with them, my grandma, and my brother. I confided in them about my situation, and they urged me to leave the farmhouse and get a lawyer. I clung to Anthony's promise that it would only be a few more months. I began visiting my parents on weekends, regaining some semblance of a normal life. Surprisingly, Anthony didn't object. This newfound contact with my family felt liberating after so long under his control.

Anthony continued to insist that I was his wife, urging me to stay strong. Almost daily, he demanded photos of me, both clothed and unclothed. At first, I complied, thinking it was harmless, but his obsession grew, with relentless requests for pictures. Reflecting now, I see it was one of his many sick obsessions, a tactic he likely used on all his girlfriends around the world.

As the holidays passed, Anthony still didn't share any pictures of Angelina or let me speak to her. He wouldn't even allow me to call him. The next time I saw him was in February, when he arrived unannounced late at night. He looked disheveled, as though he hadn't showered in days. His hair was greying, his face drawn and tired, his body emaciated. He repeated the same empty promises, urging me to stay strong for him and Angelina. Just days before his visit, I had picked up mail from our old, flooded house and found a letter in a foreign language. It revealed that Anthony owed taxes on a property in Hungary. My hands shook with rage and betrayal. The first thought that crossed my mind was that he was living with and married to Ethel.

How could someone I had loved and trusted for so many years do this to me?

The realization hit me like a tidal wave, leaving me gasping for air. Anthony had constructed an elaborate web of deceit, and I was trapped at its center. My world crumbled as the truth began to surface, and I confronted the painful reality of his betrayal and manipulation.

I snapped a quick picture of the letter with my phone before confronting Anthony. The next time he arrived at the farmhouse, I showed it to him. He snatched the letter from my hands, his face contorted with rage.

"This letter is fake!" he bellowed. "It's meant to mislead those who are after me. I'm not in Hungary; I'm much closer than you think, just a few hours away. I'm closer to you than you can imagine."

We went upstairs to the bedroom, and Anthony tried to soothe my doubts. He professed his love, telling me how much I meant to him and how soon all this would be over. His words lulled me into a fragile sense of security. We fell asleep, and for a moment, I believed him. I believed everything he told me. He left late that night, slipping back into the shadows of his secret life. The next morning, driven by a gnawing suspicion, I emailed the company whose contact information was on the letter, seeking more information. Their response came swiftly, attaching a real sales agreement in both English and Hungarian. My heart sank as I read the document, seeing Anthony and Ethel's signatures alongside a real estate attorney's details. The weight of my isolation became unbearable, and I began confiding in the other nurses at work. They urged me to go to the police and get a lawyer, but I clung to Anthony's promises, convinced they would be home in just a few more months.

By March, Anthony started visiting the farmhouse twice a week. He never stayed overnight or brought Angelina with him. He claimed he had to check in with a program every day. When I asked about Angelina, he said she was in school with other kids in the program.

"It's too dangerous to bring her along," he insisted.

The farmhouse was divided into two sections, one of which was unfinished.

"After this program, I need my own address," Anthony explained. "It's part of the rules."

He planned to fix up the other side where he would live. Despite the oddity of it, I still believed him. I helped Anthony renovate the other side of the farmhouse after work and on weekends. We laid tile in the bathrooms and installed new kitchen cabinets and counters. Anthony spent weeks meticulously working on the kitchen tiles and solid wood floors, investing more time than he ever did in his other properties. The farmhouse was transforming beautifully, and the plan was for us to live there together and rent out the other side until we bought our real home. It seemed like the perfect plan.

In April, Anthony told me he needed to complete another program called ARD—Accelerated Rehabilitative Disposition. It was typically for first-time offenders, often for DUIs, to avoid jail time.

"This will take about six months," he said. "I have to do community service to complete it."

Throughout April, Anthony claimed he was serving meals to the homeless as part of his community service. When I saw him, he looked increasingly tired and disheveled. His visits grew more distant, though he never missed a day to text me, demanding naked pictures and reminding me to pay the bills. His declarations of love felt hollow, and the prospect of six more months of waiting left me feeling utterly defeated.

Before Anthony left, he had coerced me into taking out numerous credit cards, maxing out every single one. I had to file for bankruptcy, unable to even make the minimum payments. The home equity loan was included in my bankruptcy, and the lawyer advised me to stop making payments. But I continued, fearing the loss of the farmhouse. Explaining my situation to the lawyer was humiliating. I felt terrible admitting I was divorced and that my daughter didn't live with me. I couldn't reveal that Anthony was supposedly in the witness protection program. I felt like she thought I was crazy, wasting my paycheck on a man who was never there.

I missed Angelina's fifth birthday that April. It shattered me. I had missed all the holidays with her again. I had made hotel reservations for a summer beach trip, only to cancel them. My friends at work pushed me to take action, but I still clung to the hope that they would return.

But by June, I knew I had to do something. I started looking for a lawyer, saving almost three thousand dollars by skipping mortgage payments. I scheduled a consultation with a local attorney. Pam, a good friend from work, accompanied me. I was nervous, doing something on my own for the first time. The lawyer was young and kind but didn't seem like a fighter. She suggested hiring a private investigator first. I paid her retainer fee, but over breakfast, panic set in. I rushed back to the lawyer's office, demanding my money back. She asked if Anthony had contacted me to stop this, but he didn't know. I took the cash and paid the home equity loan, feeling a twisted sense of relief, believing Anthony would be pleased.

That summer was spent working extra shifts. My paychecks were great, and I was saving for when Anthony and Angelina would return. Anthony knew I was working extra and insisted I pay the farmhouse taxes, which drained all my savings once again. Every extra dollar went to bills he demanded I pay. Despite the distance, his text messages were mean and threatening if I didn't respond quickly. He now wanted videos to verify my location. I still had to report my daily activities to him and ensure the home equity loan was paid.

I often retreated to Angelina's room, laying on her bed, crying. I rummaged through her toys, stared at her pictures, and bought her new clothes and toys. Anthony took these items each time he visited. I clung to her belongings, hoping she remembered me. Her room was filled with wrapped Christmas presents, an Easter basket, and birthday gifts. A special tooth fairy book with hidden pictures of us brought back bittersweet memories. I spent hours in the attic, going through boxes of her baby items, crying over cards and pictures from my baby shower. My sister had a baby girl in May, so I took Angelina's baby toys and furniture to my parent's house. Anthony took her old crib, claiming it was for a family in the program. He also took her baby blanket, which infuriated me as it was all I had left of her babyhood. He wasn't happy I gave the other items to my sister.

One day, I found a forgotten box containing my baptism dress and Angelina's. Seeing her dress brought back memories of her baptism—a beautiful spring day with a ceremony at the Catholic church in Hershey, PA, followed by a party at a restaurant. Anthony's ex, Natasha, was there, parading around provocatively, causing tension with Anthony's family. The day ended with Anthony telling me to pack up the gifts and take Angelina home. He later forced me to open all of Angelina's cards in front of him, his eyes burning with greed. As I peeled back each envelope, he reached over, snatching the money and shoving it into his pockets.

"No," I protested, my voice trembling with a mix of fear and anger. "The money is going into a savings account that I opened for Angelina." My gaze had flickered to her, sleeping peacefully in her car seat, oblivious to the turmoil.

In an instant, Anthony's face twisted with fury. He grabbed me by the hair and slapped my face, the sting of his hand leaving a burning imprint on my cheek. He began to knock me to the floor, his grip tightening painfully. Panic surged through me, but then, Natasha came running, her voice cutting through the chaos.

"Stop!" she had yelled, and miraculously, he did.

Weeks before the baptism, Natasha and I had been at odds, a rift Anthony had orchestrated to control us better. Now, her unexpected act of solidarity left me stunned. She walked me to the car, her eyes filled with pity.

"I'm sorry for you," she murmured, and as I drove home, leaving them to clean up after the party, a bitter realization settled in ... every good memory with Angelina was shadowed by a bad one with Anthony.

That summer felt endless, each day dragging on as I counted down to September—the month they were supposed to come home. The wait was agonizing, a relentless cycle of hope and despair. I began preparing for Angelina's return, talking to local schools to get her registered. I arranged swimming lessons, ice skating sessions, and bought Hershey Park season passes. Her closet overflowed with new clothes, a backpack, lunchbox, and countless toys. My mom sewed new curtains and quilts for her room, and Anthony told me she liked bugs, so we decided on a ladybug theme. The room was a burst of bright colors—pink, yellow, and green—a joyful space ready for her homecoming. I imagined Angelina's delight, her eyes lighting up at the sight of her new room.

One Saturday in August, I took Brigitte for a walk down the street where our old house had flooded. Passing by a house Martin had bought years ago, I noticed his truck parked outside, a sign that his tenant had moved out and he was renovating. On my way back, I saw Martin and approached him, my heart pounding with the weight of my question.

"Have you heard from Anthony? He's supposed to be coming home in September."

Martin looked down, his expression somber.

"You need to get out of that farmhouse," he said quietly. "You're young and pretty. You can marry someone else."

His words hit me like a punch to the gut. He warned me not to tell Anthony, urging me to pack up and leave.

"Anthony has started his life over. He's using you for money. You're just a paycheck to him."

"How is Angelina?" I asked, as tears welled up.

"She's in school, safe and happy," he replied. His words offered a sliver of comfort, but he wouldn't confirm their location.

"Move on with your life. Marry someone else. Get far away from Anthony," he repeated.

I thanked him for his advice, though my heart ached with confusion and sorrow. Back at the farmhouse, I decided to call Anthony's sister. When she answered, her voice was cold.

"I'm not allowed to discuss any of this with you. Don't call me ever again."

Her words cut deep. We had been close, both nurses who shared a special bond. Now, I was a stranger. Hurt and bewildered, I texted Anthony about his sister but chose not to mention my conversation with Martin.

Anthony continued to promise he'd be home in September, but then another problem arose ... he became "sick." He claimed thyroid issues had landed him in the hospital, requiring radiation therapy that confined him to a room for over a week. His story seemed plausible, and I wanted to believe him. But this excuse dragged on for three more weeks, each delay chipping away at my patience and trust.

Frustration grew, and I began to distance myself, sometimes not texting or emailing him back. I decided to call his phone, and the dial tone sounded normal—unlike the strange, distant tone from the summer, which resembled a European dial tone. Something was off. Was Anthony lying to me all this time?

The absence of my daughter for over an entire year began to erode my spirit. Depression set in, and I started to believe that Anthony might indeed be living a new life with Ethel in Hungary. I had to act, but the weight of time and lies made every step forward feel like a betrayal of my own heart. I had kept my end of the bargain, but it was clear now—I had been nothing more than a pawn in Anthony's cruel game.

···· Chapter Eleven

The days grew shorter, and the air turned crisp as autumn settled over the farmhouse. Leaves fell in golden showers, carpeting the ground in a beautiful, melancholic blanket. To brighten the place for Angelina's return, I adorned the front porch with vibrant pumpkins and large purple and yellow mums. I wanted the house to look cheerful, a warm welcome for my daughter. The date of their return had been pushed to October, and I clung to Anthony's promises like a lifeline, my hope hanging by a thread.

Anthony's daily texts were a relentless reminder of the home equity loan and other bills that needed to be paid. Since he left with Angelina, a constant, gnawing headache plagued me. I could barely eat, my weight dropping alarmingly. My hair thinned, my skin broke out, and dark circles marred my eyes from sleepless nights. Each day, I dragged myself to work, having abandoned the gym out of sheer exhaustion.

The day finally arrived. It was a Friday, and I had the day off from the hospital. I went out to buy groceries, my heart pounding with anticipation. I texted Anthony as soon as I woke up, his response laced with irritation.

"Don't you ever sleep?"

"What time are you and Angelina going to be here?" Desperation tinged my reply.

Hours passed with no response. When he finally did reply, it was to tell me to stop bothering him because he was working.

My sadness morphed into desperation, driving me to reach out to Anthony's brother's wife. She had never been unkind to me. I remembered how harshly Anthony's family judged new members, how they criticized her for staying at home without a job. Anthony's mother had often spoken negatively about her looks and fashion choices. I felt bad for her, having tried to befriend her when we lived nearby, recognizing her loneliness and depression.

I texted her, asking if she knew where my daughter was. Her reply was disheartening. She mentioned that Anthony's family was speaking ill of me, but she didn't believe everything. That was the last I heard from her; she ignored my further attempts to communicate. Her daughter and son were close in age to Angelina. *How could Anthony's entire family think it was acceptable to do this to a mother?*

In preparation for their arrival, I cooked baked ziti, chicken cutlets, and homemade pasta sauce. I decorated the dining room and bought a cake, my excitement palpable. To not have seen my daughter for over a year felt like a part of me had been ripped away. The pain was indescribable, a constant ache that left me feeling winded and heartbroken every single day.

My coworkers were my saving grace, helping me to see the situation for what it was. Katie, a colleague who had survived domestic abuse, shared her story, drawing parallels between her ex-husband and Anthony. Her resilience gave me hope that I too could find happiness, that I wasn't too old to be loved and to create the family I longed for.

As night fell on that fateful Friday, Anthony stopped answering my texts. It was eight o'clock and still no sign of them. I braced myself for another excuse, wondering what it could possibly be this time. At eleven, a loud knock echoed through the house. My heart leaped with joy. I rushed to the door, eager to finally see Angelina. *How had she grown? Would she remember me?* My mind raced with thoughts of our reunion and the plans I'd made for our weekend—a mother-daughter date at Hershey Park, shopping, and a visit to the library, her favorite place. I opened the door to find Anthony standing alone. Disappointment washed over me.

"Where is Angelina?" I asked, my voice trembling.

He claimed she was very sick and couldn't travel. He promised to bring her the next day. My face fell, unable to hide my disappointment. He asked for dinner, and I served him a plate of pasta. As he ate on the couch, he complained about feeling sick from his thyroid problems, accusing me of not caring.

"I'm sorry," I said, trying to mask my frustration. "I can help care for you at home."

After he finished eating, he sat beside me, tears glistening in his eyes. For the second time since I'd known him, he cried. His vulnerability made me believe his stories about witness protection and the ARD program. Guilt gnawed at me for not being more supportive during his supposed illness. Anthony kissed me, whispering words of love, and we went upstairs. He fell asleep, but around three in the morning, he woke in a panic. He said he had to leave, or they would come looking for him. I walked him to the front porch, where he kissed me goodbye, a hollow promise hanging in the air.

The following morning, I sent a text to Anthony, my fingers trembling as I typed. I asked how Angelina was feeling and inquired about his own health. His response was curt: she was still sick and vomiting. I had stocked up on cold medicine, Pedialyte, and foods to soothe an upset stomach, ready to care for my daughter like any devoted mother would. As the hours dragged on, I sat on the living room couch, anxiety gnawing at me. It was already evening when he finally replied, telling me they were still on their way and to stop texting him. By ten o'clock, he admitted she was too ill to travel.

This painful cycle repeated itself on Sunday and Monday. Each time, he assured me they were coming, only to send a late-night message saying Angelina was too sick. On Monday, I returned to work, dreading the questions from my coworkers who were eager to hear if my daughter was home. Breaking the news to them was devastating. Disappointment layered upon disappointment, and a chilling realization began to settle in: I might never see my daughter again.

One day, at the end of that month, I finished my shift at six in the evening. Exhausted, I returned home, grabbed a drink from the refrigerator, and my phone rang. It was Pam from work. Her voice was tense as she told me she needed to talk in person and would be at my house soon. My heart sank, suspecting it was about her recent breast cancer diagnosis.

Pam arrived within fifteen minutes, her face etched with concern and sadness. As she walked in, a gut-wrenching premonition hit me: Ethel and Anthony were together, and they had a baby. I couldn't explain it, but the thought lodged itself in my mind, filling me with dread. Pam took out her phone and showed me a picture taken by Susie, a coworker, at Saturday's Market. There was Anthony, walking with Angelina. She flipped to another photo of a woman with long brown hair pushing a baby stroller—Ethel, unmistakably. The final picture showed Anthony, Angelina, Ethel, and the baby together at the market, the very place Anthony used to take me every weekend.

My stomach twisted into knots, and I felt the urgent need to vomit. Tears streamed down my face as Pam hugged me. The truth shattered my heart into pieces. *How could someone I had been with for fourteen years do this to me? How could someone who professed to love me betray me so deeply?* Anthony had strung me along, using me for everything I had. I confessed to Pam that I had suspected this ever since Anthony had come to take Angelina's old crib, angry that I had given other baby items to my sister. That had been in the spring, and now, seeing the baby—a boy about four months old—in the pictures, the timeline made cruel sense. Pam stayed with me for a while, offering comfort as I began to formulate a plan. I needed to leave, to escape this nightmare.

Once Pam left, I called my mom, recounting the painful revelation. Relief tinged her voice at the news that I was coming home for good. The house felt like a prison as I packed my clothes, pictures, and Angelina's belongings. I left her Christmas presents, hoping Anthony would at least give them to her. Anthony never bought her new toys or clothes, a stark contrast to my constant efforts to provide.

I packed until three in the morning, adrenaline fueling my actions. Sleep was elusive, my mind racing to comprehend the betrayal. This was my chance to start over. The home equity loan was three payments behind because I had refused to pay until they were living with me. I had some cash saved in case I needed an attorney.

With barely an hour of sleep, I packed my car to the roof with my belongings. As I loaded the car, a state police officer drove by slowly. Within an hour, I received a text from Anthony, saying his state trooper friend had seen me packing and it looked like I was moving out. The realization that so many people were watching me, all loyal to Anthony, was suffocating. I drove a carload to my parents' house and returned to the farmhouse, waiting for my brother Andrew.

Andrew arrived, fresh off his shift, and together we packed the last of my things. Brigitte, my dog, squeezed into the backseat of his truck. I left the car I had been driving since it wasn't in my name. As I locked the door for the last time, a wave of bittersweet relief washed over me. No more would I have to mow the lawn, pull weeds, or maintain the property alone.

I said goodbye to the farmhouse and that chapter of my life. Packing Andrew's truck, a gut-wrenching fear lingered. What if Anthony showed up, his big truck blocking us in, trying to harm us? My main concern was for Andrew's safety. Reflecting on the past, I realized how much my relationship with Anthony had hurt my family, particularly Andrew. He had been just ten years old when I started dating Anthony and had witnessed my transformation over the years, the distance I had created between myself and our family.

Anthony must have been far away, or he would have tried to stop me. His texts came in rapid succession, but I ignored them. I left every picture of us on the dining room table, a symbolic gesture of letting go. Anthony had built a life with Ethel, and I was done being part of his deceit. As I drove away, a sense of liberation mixed with the pain of betrayal. The truth had finally come out, and I was ready to reclaim my life.

All I was to Anthony was a paycheck and a groundskeeper, maintaining the property while he lived his new life in Hungary. He had this new life planned for over two years, when I first tried to leave him. *How could someone think it's acceptable to separate a mother from her child and brainwash that child into believing another woman is her mother?* I will never understand.

It was Halloween, the day my new life began. The feeling was surreal. For the first time in years, I didn't have the suffocating panic that Anthony instilled in me. Returning to him was not an option. What was I supposed to do—live with his new wife Ethel like we were in some polygamist setup? Absurd. That day, I fell completely out of love with him.

I received a chilling text from Anthony.

"Martin has changed all the locks, and you are hereby notified not to enter the farmhouse anymore. Call if you forgot anything."

Later that evening, he sent pictures of Angelina. One was of her in a witch costume from when she was three, clearly taken from her old closet at the farmhouse. He was taunting me, letting me know they were back home.

I replied, telling him to leave me alone, pointing out that he had a new life and a baby with Ethel. He denied the baby's existence but continued sending me pictures of Angelina. For over a year, he had refused to send photos or let me talk to her, claiming he wasn't allowed due to being in witness protection. Yet now, in one evening, he flooded me with images, proving he was never in such a program. Witness protection rules strictly prohibit contact with former associates or returning to one's old town.

The next day, I contacted my lawyer, Devra, and set up a consultation. I was determined to get my child back. Anthony had dismissed my previous threats to get a lawyer, but this time, I had saved enough money by not paying the home equity loan. I was ready for the retainer fee.

In the following days, Anthony sent more texts, trying to undermine my resolve.

"Last time you got a lawyer, it didn't work. It was a waste of money," he taunted, attaching a picture of Angelina with a bunny.

He professed his love, saying I was special to him. The baby's existence gnawed at me, and I texted back.

"You have a new family and baby!" He tried calling, but I didn't answer. I sent him the picture of Ethel and the baby. He couldn't deny it anymore. Knowing I had a lawyer, he would try his hardest to make me drop the case and return to him.

Determined, I reached out to Ethel's ex-boyfriend, Dave, on Facebook. To my surprise, he responded. He recounted meeting Anthony three years ago at a house party. Ethel, desperate for a job, was enthralled by Anthony's wealth and charm. She started working for him, and soon, their relationship grew closer. Dave noticed Ethel spending more time with Anthony, often picked up in his expensive cars. Eventually, Dave kicked her out of his apartment, suspecting her involvement with Anthony. Homeless, Ethel moved in with Anthony at a secret apartment in the city, a place I knew nothing about.

Dave revealed that Anthony's control over Ethel was manipulative. He would throw her out during arguments, only to take her back later. This cycle continued until Dave decided to cut ties with Ethel entirely. He stayed in touch with Ethel's cousin, who mentioned their plan to travel between Hungary and the US. The following summer, Dave saw Ethel, Anthony, and Angelina at a mall. Anthony, recognizing Dave, hurriedly left the scene. This was around the time they changed their phone plans for international use.

Dave agreed to meet me at the hospital where I worked to share more details. He described how Anthony had taken Ethel from him and how much it hurt. Despite Ethel's attempts to leave Anthony, something kept her bound to him. Dave remembered the address of the secret apartment, which turned out to be owned by one of Anthony's close friends, someone I used to babysit for. *Why were these people covering for Anthony? What leverage did he have over them?*

When I first met Anthony, I never imagined he was capable of such deceit. His daughter had warned me when I was pregnant to take Angelina and run, advice I now regretted not heeding. I wished I had recognized the signs of abuse and been stronger. The few good times we had never lasted, overshadowed by the countless tough times. Now, I was ready to fight for my daughter. This was my time to reclaim our lives, and I was prepared for the battle ahead.

···Chapter Twelve

I lay alone on my bed in my childhood bedroom, enveloped in the comforting quilt my mom had sewn. The familiar fabric was a small solace as I tried to comprehend the whirlwind of events that had upended my life. Brigitte, my loyal dog, sensed my turmoil and jumped onto the bed, pressing her nose against my feet. She stayed close, her presence a balm for my aching heart. Dogs have an uncanny ability to offer unconditional love, especially during the darkest times. Brigitte's warmth and loyalty provided an anchor amidst the storm of trauma and heartbreak I was enduring.

How could someone I had known and loved for fourteen years betray me so profoundly?

It was a question that haunted me, a relentless echo in my mind. Anthony had professed love and care, yet his actions were a stark contradiction. I needed a week off work just to begin processing the magnitude of it all. My sole focus became getting my daughter back, and I knew I had to establish firm boundaries. I vowed not to be drawn back into Anthony's manipulative orbit as I had been the last time I sought legal action.

Blocking him out entirely wasn't an option, as my lawyer Devra had a plan. This was a fragile, precarious time, and I leaned heavily on my support system. For over a decade, it had been drilled into me to trust only Anthony. Stepping away from that ingrained belief and surrounding myself with loved ones who nurtured my mental health was a monumental step.

In a desperate move, I decided to call Anthony's uncle, who lived in Pennsylvania near Anthony's mother. To my relief, he picked up and agreed to talk. I poured out my confusion and pain, explaining that I had a lawyer and was determined to see my daughter again. He revealed that Anthony and Ethel planned to live in the US for six months and in Hungary for the other six. He empathized with my hurt and offered to pray with me. Before we ended the call, he warned.

"Anthony is very good in court, and some of the accusations he has against you will be tough to fight."

Strangely, this only fueled my resolve. Despite knowing me for years, his family easily turned against me, fully supporting Anthony.

Devra's first plan was to hire a private investigator to gather evidence that Angelina was physically in the United States. At the time, I don't think Devra fully believed that Anthony was traveling internationally and owned property in Hungary. Anthony continuously sent me pictures and videos of Angelina, trying to undermine my resolve. The most painful video was of Angelina walking near a swimming pool, with Anthony and Ethel's voices in the background. I could hear Ethel talking.

"Angelina, my daughter," followed by her laughter. It was a cruel stab to my heart.

Other pictures showed Angelina in front of expensive Mercedes wagons, at the circus, and among children at a school or church. After over a year of no contact, this sudden influx of images was bewildering and painful. Anthony was pulling out all the stops to make me drop my lawyer and return to him.

By late November, I was on call at the hospital for the weekend after Thanksgiving. Devra's strategy involved keeping communication with Anthony open to set up a meeting to see Angelina, allowing the private investigator to get pictures. I knew this would be challenging, as Anthony was no novice in custody battles. I feigned interest in dropping my lawyer, trying to lure Anthony into a meeting.

That Saturday, I was working on a call case at the hospital when I texted Anthony, saying I could be at the farmhouse soon. As I pulled into the driveway, I noticed a white Volkswagen Jetta parked there—Ethel's car. A wave of nausea hit me. The door to the other side of the house was wide open, and I could hear someone working inside. Reluctantly, I called out Anthony's name. A tall, foreign-looking blonde man emerged, his expression blank and unwelcoming. He didn't speak English, and my attempts to communicate were futile.

I walked back to my car, shaken. Moments later, Anthony arrived in his tow truck, a smile plastered on his face. He looked dreadful with an overgrown, unkempt beard streaked with gray and black. His clothes were filthy and tattered. He invited me inside, where the other man was working, but wouldn't explain who he was beyond being a worker. Apparently, Anthony had promised him the Jetta if he finished the job.

I had no interest in seeing the farmhouse's progress. It was no longer our future home, no longer a place for the family of three we were supposed to be. This encounter solidified my resolve—I would fight with every ounce of strength I had to reclaim my daughter and break free from Anthony's grasp once and for all.

Seeing all the hard work we had poured into the farmhouse brought a deep, aching sadness. I had truly believed that it would be our home, a place where we would build our future together. As Anthony led me to the other side of the farmhouse, memories flooded back. Everything was still in place, untouched. The furniture, my clothes—everything remained as I had left it. When Anthony pointed out that I had left many of my belongings, I simply told him I didn't want any of it. We sat down next to each other on the couch, the weight of unspoken words heavy in the air.

"Where is Angelina?" I asked, my voice barely a whisper. He avoided my gaze, refusing to answer. Instead, he looked into my eyes.

"I love you and will always love you."

It was surreal. *How could he think that he could keep me, pretend we had a relationship, while living a double life?* He then showed me residency cards for Hungary, his and Angelina's. He painted a picture of a rich, lavish lifestyle, flying to Italy on weekends, promising I'd never have to work again if I joined him. But then, almost in the same breath, he shifted.

"Are you going to continue making payments on the farmhouse?" He suggested that if I didn't want to move to Hungary, I could just stay there.

None of it made sense. *If he had so much money, why did he care about the payments?* I saw through his lies for the first time. He tried to convince me that the home equity loan on the farmhouse wasn't part of my bankruptcy, but I knew better.

While we were inside, Susie and Katie were outside, working to place the tracker. They parked down the street, and Katie stayed with the car while Susie approached the farmhouse. Timing her move with the loud noise of a circular saw being used by a man outside, Susie managed to attach the tracker under the car. The loud thud it made worried her, but the man seemed oblivious, continuing his work.

Back inside, the emotional strain was too much, and I began to cry. Though I wasn't scared of physical harm from Anthony anymore, the emotional manipulation was overwhelming. As I sat on the bottom of the stairs, Anthony knelt, placing his hands on my legs and his forehead against mine, murmuring that everything would be okay. It was a familiar tactic, one he had used before, but the words felt hollow. I played along, hugging him back, and soon we were kissing. He kept telling me how much he missed me, how he missed my cooking and being with me. We went upstairs, but this time it was different. There was no feeling, only emptiness. I wondered if this was how he felt with everyone he slept with.

Afterwards, I got dressed, eager to leave. Before I could, Anthony grabbed my phone, trying to forward emails from Devra to himself. He managed to send a couple before I wrested it back. I kissed him goodbye and left, feeling disgusted with myself. I had used him, and it felt dirty and gross. When I got home, I tried to hook up the tracking device, but it wouldn't work. I spent all night trying, to no avail.

The next day, I got called in to work at the hospital for an emergency. I texted Anthony, asking to meet again. He insisted on the farmhouse. Susie and Katie planned to retrieve the tracker. Anthony and I talked more about moving to Hungary. He said I'd need a new passport because he had "lost" my old one. He suggested meeting at JFK airport to fly over together, claiming it was no big deal for him to travel back and forth. His expectations were absurd.

He tried to convince me he had taken a picture of the private investigator I had hired. I agreed with everything he said, keeping him happy. After I left, he drove off in his tow truck. Katie tried to follow but lost him on the highway. The next day, Katie and her son saw Anthony working at the farmhouse again. Her son managed to retrieve the tracker, but it was useless. Time was running out, and I feared they would leave the country soon. I informed Devra that we needed to act quickly. On the following Monday, I received an email from her stating that the judge had signed an order requiring Anthony to surrender Angelina's passport and not take her out of the county. It was a glimmer of hope, but Anthony still hadn't been served the papers.

Anthony had changed. Once meticulous about his appearance, he now had a messy beard, grey hair, deep wrinkles, and shabby clothes. The stress was evident. Every night, I prayed for my daughter's safe return, for her happiness and health, and for justice. The pain of having my child ripped away was unbearable.

That December, Anthony sent one last picture of Angelina, smiling with an orange drink in front of her. She had my eyes and smile, and I hoped he noticed that every day. His last text asked if I would give him the boots and skates I had bought for Angelina. I offered to bring them if I could see her, but he never replied. I missed another year of holidays with my daughter. Devra sent letters to his PO box, but he fled to Hungary before being officially served.

Fortunately, we had a custody conference scheduled for my upcoming birthday. It felt like a sign of hope in this relentless battle.

··· Chapter Thirteen

It was a cold and frigid January morning, the kind that cuts through even the warmest layers. The sky was a clear, piercing blue, but the air had a raw chill that bit at my cheeks. My parents and I walked from the parking garage to the courthouse, bundled in our winter coats, scarves, and gloves. The walk felt interminable, though it was only a couple of blocks. Winter was never my favorite season, and on this day, it felt particularly harsh. As we made our way through courthouse security and up the elevators to the third floor, my anxiety grew with each step. We sat on the hard wooden benches, waiting for the scheduled conference to discuss when I could see Angelina again. The irony was not lost on me that it was my thirty-second birthday. My friend Susie from work sat with us, offering silent support.

Devra, my attorney, arrived shortly after. Each time I entered that county courthouse, a wave of dread washed over me. It was a place that felt alien, where fear and anxiety were my constant companions. The thought of Anthony showing up filled me with a visceral fear, even though I knew I was safe inside. *But what about the walk back to the parking garage?*

The meeting began, but Anthony never showed. As Devra and I entered the conference room, she explained the situation to the court officer. The same lady who had been there when I unknowingly signed the divorce papers greeted us. She recognized me immediately, commenting that my case had stood out among the hundreds she handled. It was a small, bittersweet validation.

Towards the end of the meeting, the court officer mentioned that we could file for emergency relief, yet the complication remained—Anthony had never been officially served with the papers to modify custody. They scheduled an emergency hearing, and the judge granted us permission to serve Anthony by email, ordering him to keep his email open and active. It was a small victory in an otherwise uphill battle.

Soon after, Anthony hired a lawyer, one who had previously worked with our judge. This conflict of interest led to another rescheduling of the emergency hearing, now set for February, with a different judge. The private investigator had served Anthony's mother and his business partner Martin as witnesses. All I could do was wait. Anthony's lawyer confirmed that he was in Hungary, but refused to provide an address. My daily texts, Skype messages, and emails to Anthony, pleading to speak with Angelina, went unanswered. The silence was deafening.

One weekday, towards the end of my shift at the hospital, my boss approached me, asking if we could meet with someone from Human Resources. Panic set in.

"Am I in trouble?" I asked.

"Oh no, you're not in trouble," she reassured me. My boss knew about my struggles with Anthony. Her eyes welled with tears, and I tried to comfort her.

"If this is about my ex-husband, I will get through it."

In a conference room upstairs, we met Ashley from Human Resources. She explained that Anthony had sent emails and pictures, trying to use old text messages against me. These were desperate messages I had sent, saying I wanted to kill myself, hoping to get a response from him when he claimed to be in witness protection with Angelina. It wasn't my finest moment, but I had been desperate. Ashley reassured me that this was a standard procedure to ensure my safety. Anthony was trying to sabotage me, to get me fired so I couldn't afford to pay Devra. She mentioned an incident when Anthony had harassed me at the hospital, and the police had to be called. I had never pressed charges. After the meeting, I called Devra. Anthony had not only contacted my workplace but had also made calls to the main Penn State campus and other hospital outlets. Devra decided to subpoena Ashley as a witness for the upcoming court hearing.

The following day, my bankruptcy lawyer emailed me, saying Anthony had accused me of fraud. Devra intervened, and all I had to do was update my address and expense list. Anthony's attempts to unsettle me were relentless. With the court hearing approaching, I sought counseling to help me cope and understand my emotions. I felt numb, as if all of this was happening to someone else. Talking to friends and family, especially those who had experienced abusive relationships, provided some solace.

The night before the hearing, Devra and I prepped for hours. She informed me that Anthony's original lawyer had dropped him, and he now had a reputable new lawyer. I needed to be prepared for a tough cross-examination. Despite my nerves, I slept well that night. Staying strong was imperative, and I focused on healthy eating and exercise to manage my stress. Counseling helped me accept that my emotions would be a rollercoaster. Some days I felt strong and confident in my decision to leave, while other days I was overwhelmed by sadness and anxiety. The counselor assured me that these feelings were normal and that survival, not immediate healing, was my priority after leaving an abusive relationship.

As I braced myself for the hearing, I knew that my journey was far from over, but I was determined to fight for my daughter and for justice. On the day of the hearing, my parents drove me to the courthouse. The drive was silent, the weight of the impending confrontation pressing down on us. We parked in the garage down the street and walked over to the courthouse. I wore a navy-blue suit that hung loosely on my frame, my hair pulled back in a low ponytail. The suit, a size 0, was still too big; I had lost so much weight from the stress that I had to use safety pins to hold my pants up.

As we approached the courthouse, I couldn't help but notice its imposing grandeur. The large pillars, granite steps, and a beautiful fountain with a massive marble statue of a man with his right arm raised all felt surreal. It was as if the building itself was a testament to the significance of the battles fought within its walls. We walked through the front door, passing through metal detectors and security. The main lobby's red marble walls added to the overwhelming sense of gravity.

We took the elevator to the fifth floor and were directed to wait outside courtroom number seven. Sitting on a bench with my parents, I felt the weight of the moment pressing down on me. I peeked into the courtroom; the redwood walls, etched glass windows, and gold carvings made it look both majestic and intimidating. The front wall, seemingly made entirely of marble, added to the atmosphere of solemnity. Everything felt so overwhelming and scary at the same time. I reminded myself that this was a safe place, that these people were here to hear my story and help me. I practiced deep breathing exercises to calm my nerves, knowing that entering a courthouse for such a personal and emotional hearing is an experience that leaves an indelible mark.

As I sat there, trying to maintain my composure, I reminded myself to remain respectful and composed. I handed my phone to my parents, wanting to ensure I was fully present in the moment. The judge had granted that it was okay for Anthony to testify via Skype, which led to a change in plans—the hearing would now take place in a conference room. My friends from work, Susie and Katie, arrived first and sat next to my parents. Their presence was a balm to my anxiety and nervousness. This was my first time in a courtroom, having to be questioned by a lawyer, but

I took a few deep breaths, reassuring myself that it would be okay.

As I returned from the bathroom, I saw Anthony's business partner, Martin, approaching my parents. He spoke loudly.

"What's going on? When is this starting? Are we ready?"

He didn't realize they were my parents. I walked up behind him and smiled; he sat back down on the bench across from them, looking nervous, pale, and sweating. He never thought I would take it this far, believing I would give up. His oversized black suit seemed to swallow him whole. Anthony's mom arrived next and sat down next to Martin, avoiding eye contact with me. She knew deep down that everything that had happened was wrong.

Finally, the lawyers arrived. Devra carried so many files that she needed a suitcase binder on wheels. We all walked into the conference room, and I felt a sense of relief. The smaller room was less intimidating, more comfortable. The judge sat at the head of the conference table, her laptop set up and ready. A police officer sat to her left. Devra and I sat to her right, with a sonographer beside me. The sonographer was kind, sharing stories about her daughter who was also a nurse. Her friendliness made the situation a bit more bearable.

Anthony's lawyer, Pat, and his young assistant sat across from us. Pat, probably in his late fifties didn't seem intimidating, but his assistant struggled to set up the Skype connection. Finally, everything was ready. My family, friends, and the witnesses waited outside the room. The hearing was about to begin. I sat with my hands crossed on the table, sitting up straight, trying to project confidence and attentiveness.

The judge rose to speak.

"We will issue the briefing schedule."

Pat immediately stood up.

"I guess my only thought on that, which I would like on the record, is given that we have objected to the jurisdiction and given that my client is, and we are prepared to present evidence that my client is living in Hungary and has been living in Hungary since July of 2016. If the court doesn't have jurisdiction of this case, it would not be appropriate for the Court to move forward to address the substantive issues raised in the petition that was filed."

"Right," the judge responded. "So, we will just take the testimony today from everybody. Then I rule and then we will have an order, or we don't have an order."

Pat and his assistant continued to struggle with the Skype connection, which made them appear unprepared. The judge even remarked that a trial run should have been conducted before the hearing. Finally, the connection was established, and we were ready to proceed.

The judge looked at Devra.

"Okay. So, this is a petition for special relief that was filed by you."

"Yes," she replied. The judge explained,

"I will permit both of you to use the same technique we use in custody trials and support trials, which is giving me an offer of proof, background information, so you don't need to ask your client each simple question," the judge explained.

"Then you can ask them individual questions on things that are critical or if there are special issues related to," he continued. "So, please listen to your counsel very carefully because she is going to be giving the long offer of proof, background information, and then we are going to ask you if this is correct. Okay?"

As the hearing began, I felt a mix of fear and hope. The room, though smaller, was still a battleground for my future and that of my daughter. I knew I had to stay strong, to fight for what was right, and to tell my story with the clarity and conviction it deserved.

Devra started out with the background information stating, "Rebecca resides at Shermans Dale, Pennsylvania. She has been residing there since approximately November 2017. She is the mother of Angelina born in 2012 who is now age 5. The father of the child is Anthony who is last known to reside at Hummelstown, PA, Dauphin County, Pennsylvania. His last known address with the court was a P.O. Box Hershey, PA."

"Mother filed a petition for modification of the existing custody order on November 30th of 2017 and she also simultaneously filed a petition for special relief to request that the father not remove the child from Central Pennsylvania pending disposition of her petition for modification and she requested that father turn over the child's passport. An order was entered by a judge on November 30th of 2017 in fact directing the father to not remove the child from Central Pennsylvania and to immediately surrender the child's passport to the court and that order was signed. A copy of that order was sent to Anthony at P.O. Box Hershey, PA by me, Rebecca's attorney, marked unclaimed. I also sent the same packet which contained the petition for modification, petition for special relief, and judge's order on that same date to him first class mail. The first-class mail was never returned to me but again the certified mail did come back unclaimed."

"A custody conciliation was held. Anthony did not show up and then this hearing was scheduled. My client alleges in her petition that the child has continuously resided in Pennsylvania since August 13th of 2015. There has been a pattern of the father removing the child from her mother since entry of the last custody order."

"Following the last proceeding in August 2015 the child went to live with her mother at the farmhouse property that is deeded to father, but that mother and father resided at. Rebecca resided there with the child and the father stayed there from time to time. He would often times stay at his restaurant which was located in Shipoke and the child could be with mother at all times unless she was working, and when she was working which she is a nurse at Hershey Medical Center, when she was working, father would have custody and allege that he would keep the child at his restaurant but would never permit mother to. So, from August 13, 2015, and continuing to approximately July of 2016 father would keep the child more than mother. He insisted that mother should work more and so she picked up shifts at the hospital and worked there in the evenings and during the day which resulted in father having the child more and more. There came a point where father would not even bring the child on a regular basis and then by July of 2016, he stopped bringing her altogether."

"Now we do have evidence that my client did find, because this is a very complex fact pattern, of the child being at the farmhouse August 1st of 2016. So that was the last time she saw her child. After that father stopped bringing the child to mother altogether and would make up one excuse after the other."

Devra continued to go through my entire story, including Anthony's claim that he was in a witness protection program. That he had tricked me into giving up custody of my daughter to keep her safe. That he continued to ask me to make sexy movies to send to him, and his patterns of coercion through our 14 years together.

Devra continued, "All the while my client obviously is talking to her friends and family about what she is going through regarding not being able to see her child and lo and behold one of her co-workers who is our witness today was at the Saturday's Market in Middletown and sees Anthony with the child. And, also, his wife. Her name is Ethel. I have an affidavit to that effect. And this was October 28th of 2017 when Susie was at the Saturday's Market and saw Anthony with the child Angelina and another woman who my client will testify in the pictures as Ethel, Anthony's wife, walking through the Saturday's Market. Susie took pictures, gave them to Rebecca and Rebecca realized at this point that Anthony has been stringing her along lying and that he is never going to bring this child back to her and so what she did is she moved out of the farmhouse. She packed up all her things."

"Following that we filed our custody action because we are seeking to modify the order. She is realizing that Anthony is never going to let her see this little girl again. She regrets agreeing to this order. She trusted him. She thought that he needed help. There is a 14-year history of this man convincing her to do things in a very what I would consider abusive fashion mentally and physically. He has a history of physically harming her, threatening her job, threatening her well-being and she was scared of him and believed anything he said and trusted him and thought that she was doing the right thing when she agreed to entry of this order, and it turns out that he has no intention of ever letting her see the child again." Pat stood up and yelled, "Objection as to what it turns out!"

Devra continued, "So, following our filing of the petition for modification and petition for special relief Anthony has in fact continued—" Again Pat yelled, "I am going to object to what Anthony may have done that she found objectionable unless it directly relates to the child. Devra responded, "Well, it does. Rebecca has consistently asked to talk to the child. He will not allow it. She has sent messages, Skype, text messages. I messaged him in between time where he had said he had one attorney and then another. He would not respond to any of those. He has also contacted a bankruptcy trustee in her bankruptcy action that she filed." Pat replied, "I am going to object to the relevancy of him contacting the bankruptcy judge unless it directly relates to the child."

Devra began with a calm yet determined voice, setting the stage with critical background information.

"Rebecca resides in Shermans Dale, Pennsylvania, and has been living there since approximately November 2017. She is the mother of Angelina, born in 2012, who is now five years old. The father, Anthony, was last known to reside in Hummelstown, PA, Dauphin County. His last known address with the court was a P.O. Box in Hershey, PA."

With each word, the tension in the room seemed to grow thicker. I could feel my heart pounding in my chest as Devra meticulously laid out the facts.

"Mother filed a petition for modification of the existing custody order on November 30, 2017, and simultaneously filed a petition for special relief. She requested that the father not remove the child from Central Pennsylvania pending the disposition of her petition for modification and that he turn over the child's passport. An order was entered by a judge on November 30, 2017, directing the father not to remove the child from Central Pennsylvania and to immediately surrender the child's passport to the court. That order was signed, and a copy sent to Anthony's P.O. Box in Hershey, PA by me, Rebecca's attorney. The mail was marked unclaimed. The same packet, containing the petition for modification, petition for special relief, and judge's order, was sent via first-class mail. The first-class mail was never returned, but the certified mail came back unclaimed."

I could feel the eyes in the room shifting towards me, filled with empathy and curiosity. Devra continued, her voice unwavering.

"A custody conciliation was held, but Anthony did not show up, leading to the scheduling of this hearing. My client alleges in her petition that the child has continuously resided in Pennsylvania since August 13, 2015. There has been a pattern of the father removing the child from her mother since the entry of the last custody order."

The room was silent, every word hanging heavily in the air.

"Following the last proceeding in August 2015, the child went to live with her mother at the farmhouse property deeded to the father, where both parents had resided. Rebecca lived there with the child while the father stayed there intermittently. He often stayed at his restaurant in Shipoke, allowing the child to be with her mother unless she was working. Rebecca, a nurse at Hershey Medical Center, would leave the child with the father during her shifts. From August 13, 2015, to approximately July 2016, the father increasingly kept the child, insisting Rebecca work more. Eventually, by July 2016, he stopped bringing the child to her altogether."

Devra's recounting brought back a flood of memories, each more painful than the last.

"We have evidence that my client last saw her child at the farmhouse on August 1, 2016. After that, the father stopped bringing the child to the mother entirely, making up excuses each time."

The courtroom felt smaller as Devra delved deeper into the story, revealing the layers of manipulation and deceit.

"Anthony claimed to be in a witness protection program, tricking Rebecca into giving up custody to keep their daughter safe. He continued to coerce her over their fourteen-year relationship, asking for explicit videos and employing various forms of mental and physical abuse."

My heart ached as Devra spoke, each word a reminder of the nightmare I had lived through.

"Rebecca spoke to her friends and family about her ordeal. One of our witnesses today, a co-worker, saw Anthony with the child and another woman at Saturday's Market in Middletown. This was on October 28, 2017. Susie, our witness, took pictures and shared them with Rebecca, revealing that Anthony had been lying all along. Realizing he had no intention of bringing the child back, Rebecca moved out of the farmhouse, packing up all her things."

Devra's narration painted a vivid picture of my desperation and determination.

"Following that, we filed our custody action, seeking to modify the order. Rebecca realized Anthony would never let her see her daughter again. She regretted agreeing to the initial order, having trusted him out of fear and manipulation. Over their fourteen-year history, Anthony had convinced her to do things through abusive tactics, both mentally and physically. He had threatened her job, her well-being, and she believed she was doing the right thing by agreeing to the order."

The courtroom was electric with anticipation as Pat, Anthony's lawyer, stood up abruptly.

"Objection as to what it turns out!"

Devra, unshaken, continued.

"Following our filing of the petition for modification and petition for special relief, Anthony has continued—"

Pat interrupted again.

"I am going to object to what Anthony may have done that she found objectionable unless it directly relates to the child."

Devra's voice remained steady.

"It does. Rebecca has consistently asked to talk to the child. He will not allow it. She has sent messages via Skype, text, and I have messaged him as well, but he responds with excuses, changing attorneys, and avoiding communication. He even contacted a bankruptcy trustee in her bankruptcy action to complicate matters further."

Pat interjected once more.

"I am going to object to the relevancy of him contacting the bankruptcy judge unless it directly relates to the child."

The judge listened intently, the air thick with the gravity of the situation. It was clear that this was more than a legal battle; it was a fight for justice and the truth, a fight for my daughter, and a fight for my life.

"Well, it does because it's a pattern of his threats and she had taken this home equity line of equity for him on his farm property to help him out," Devra said back to Pat

Again, Pat yelled.

"I am objecting to relevance. Again, she may not be happy with things that happened between them financially, but it's not relevant in the custody case!"

Devra quickly responded.

"He contacted them and accused her of fraud right after we filed our petition for modification."

"Objection. Relevance." Pat said in a monotone voice. The judge said,

"If he is accusing her of fraud, it shows a pattern of behavior," the judge said.

"Unless she had engaged in fraud," Pat replied.

"Truth would be a defense," the judge responded.

Devra continued.

"He also contacted her employer and made multiple complaints to her employer and sent what we believe to be very old or made-up images of my client doing things. She works for Hershey Med. She is a nurse and he made multiple complaints. One was a verbal complaint. There were several—",

"I need a foundation on this," Pat annoyingly responded.

"It talked about custody," Devra replied. "It talked about how crazy she was." Again, Pat stated,

"I need a foundation on how it is that your client knows that Anthony made complaints because if it is based on what somebody said to her …"

"The witness is here." Pat tried to brush it off saying,

"Then that is hearsay. So, if you have a witness…"

"Who is this person going to be?" The judge was interested to know.

"Her name is Ashley. She is here from Penn State from the Employee Relations Department," Devra answered. The judge asked Devra,

"Okay, anything else from your client at this point?"

"Yes. I do have a few other points. Anthony is claiming that he has been living in Hungary since July of 2016. We have evidence that the child was here in August of 2016 with a picture of her at the farmhouse. We also have evidence that he went to Dewey Beach with Rebecca in August 2016. She paid for the tickets. It was supposed to be a family trip with Angelina. He showed up without Angelina, claimed Angelina was at his mom's house and he went to the beach with my client."

"And where does the mom live?" the judge asked Devra.

"His mom lives in Lititz, PA and she is subpoenaed to be here. She was personally served. Your Honor, I am just trying to make sure I have hit everything. I also wanted to make sure that to continue her offer of proof that when she was at the farmhouse with the child from August 15, 2015, through July of 2016 the child had a bedroom there. She took the child to the library, checked out books, took her places, did things with her and when she believed that Anthony was bringing the child back, signed her up for swimming lessons, got her Hershey Park passes and made Anthony aware of all that."

The hearing started out very intense. It was constantly back and forth between the lawyers, and they were getting loud and heated. The judge said that she wanted to start out with my friend Susie as the first witness to be called in. The exhibits that we had were the pictures that she took at Saturday's Market of Anthony, Ethel, and Angelina. Pat said that he has no objection of those pictures and that he does not have any cross examination on it. He didn't want to spend time on it. These pictures showed how Anthony was lying to me. Susie did not have to come into the court room.

Ashley was called in next as a witness with direct examination by Devra. She was asked questions like where are your employed at? And what is your position there? As soon as Devra asked her, "Did you have a meeting with Rebecca a couple weeks ago regarding complaints that you received about her." Pat stood up and said, "I am going to object at this point to the relevance of testimony regarding any reporting that was made by my client or others with regard to Rebecca and her fitness to serve as a registered nurse. If he had done that, I don't know how it's relevant to the custody proceedings. I believe the underlying concerns are relevant. I don't know if you have page D-18 in front of you." The judge said, "I have nothing."

Pat continued, "This is also a picture that we will be presenting of Rebecca in a noose threatening to kill herself and I believe that my client may very well have reported to Hershey Medical Center that one of their RN's was mentally unstable and felt that they should know that. I don't know how that is relevant to this custody case. The underlying mental health issues are certainly relevant to the custody but not the reporting of that, I do not know if that is relevant."

Devra asked the judge, "Your Honor, if I can respond. The reporting of this to Penn State is relevant because it shows his efforts to retaliate against my client for anything she is going to do to try to seek custodial rights for her child and he talks about the custody case within this document. He makes statements with this document about a hearing that happened January 30th, 2018, which did not go as she expected."

Devra continued to ask Ashley more questions, "When was that meeting? And what was the nature of this meeting?" Ashley responded,

"So the nature of that meeting was for me to meet Rebecca as well as to ensure that she was in a safe place and that the concerns that were noted about her for me to basically ensure that there weren't any concerns for her safety at the time that I met with her."

Devra asked Ashley, "And what did you determine?" Ashley said, "I was very comfortable. She was coherent. We talked about the things that he reported, and their derogatory nature and she acknowledged that she was aware that that might be coming and that she anticipated that there would be reporting done."

Devra asked Ashley, "So when you say complaints he makes, could you explain to the Court what complaints you received and what they essentially were indicating?" Ashley answered, "Sure. So, the first complaint came in through what we call our HR Solutions Center. It's a place where, it is an open phone number that anyone can call, employees or outside, and it was roughly a twenty-minute phone call, and I provided the summary that the HR Solutions Center gave to me, but it was from this gentleman Anthony, and he was stating that he was concerned for her safety." He was concerned for her safety and one of the concerns that I had was that if he was concerned for her safety why did he wait eight days to call from the incident which he told us he was concerned. As part of that, you know, we recommend that they contact the police if someone is concerned for safety of which he had told us, there is a twenty-minute phone call, we have it recorded, that didn't happen and so that was the first point of contact."

"The first complaint had come in February 6th and then subsequently a complaint was made through our compliance department. February 8th, 2018, this is a written complaint. It's the fourth page and the top email, well it was from my director with forwarding the concern to my attention. The complaint was made in writing and was very similar to the telephone call."

Devra asked Ashley, "What was the nature of the complaint?" She answered, "Just, well, claiming that she could or, I am sorry, can take drugs at home, not that she takes drugs at home and that basically that she has access but of course our nurses have access to medication and then he went into this long history of his, you know, account of her medical and mental states, situations that have happened with another ex-girlfriend or something of that nature. I mean, talked about the custody case."

Devra asked, "Was there a complaint received after that?" Ashley said, "I received it on the 8th in the evening, however, it actually came in on the 7th in the evening of February. So, he used the patient complaint service to then essentially recap up to 5,000 characters per complaint. So essentially its almost cut and paste verbatim from the first complaint."

Devra asked Ashley how these complaints came in. Ashley explained that the first one was both web and portal systems. The first one came though the web portal that goes directly to their compliance officers who then route it to human resources. This one came through patient services and then patient services reported it though patient safety who then came to HR. On February 9th of 2018 they received a report. She said that this one was an email to one of the employees at Penn State main campus at the university and so that was through their office of ethics and compliance and so they forwarded it to their compliance department.

Devra continued to ask her what was the nature of this complaint? Ashley explained that it was the same accounting of my health history, our court history, custody history, and again that I had access to drugs but no definite report that I take them or have ever claimed to take them or anything.

Devra asked Ashley if there were any attachments to these emails. Ashley explained that he attached the text message that he had already sent to her but this time he added picture messages. They were pictures of me. She explained that it was one of those things that she needed to validate. Anthony had screen shot that it was on the first but again based on the kind of the escalation of reporting though multiple avenues. Anthony kept on adding pieces of this reporting. Three days later she said they got pictures that they didn't have the first day or the first report. Ashley wanted to validate that this wasn't a current situation. Devra asked Manda if there were any dates on the pictures? She replied, "Again, no. There were dates from what we saw from the screen shot but they were not provided in any of the previous complaints."

Next was cross examination by Pat to Ashley. Pat asked Ashley what her role in this was when she interviewed me. She responded, "Not to interview her, no. I was meeting with her." He questioned her, "You met with her?" Ashley replied, "To check on her well-being to make sure that everything was okay and that she was in a good place and safe because I was concerned about her safety."

Pat continued to ask, "And was that the extent of your involvement in this matter, receiving complaints and being with Rebecca?" Ashley answered, "Met with her to ensure her safety, yes. And we did a validation in the background narcotic use, but it was fine and checked out fine. So, she had appropriate narcotic use, appropriate narcotic wasting. So, we did validate that as a precaution but there were no concerns when we validated her drug pulls and administration which is why my concern was not wasting or her taking medication. My concern was her safety." Pat was done with his cross examination of Ashley.

Devra continued to ask Ashley, "As a result of these multiple complaints that you received by Anthony against Rebecca, was there any referral made to the Department of State? She answered, "There was not. No, we have no concerns about her practice." Devra questioned Ashley, "And in your experience did you find it unusual the number of complaints in the short duration of time that your received against this employee?" Ashley replied, "Yes, and that was one of my concerns more than anything for her safety because it seemed as if there was escalation. When the first response didn't, I mean over a course of three days if you are worried about somebody's safety, typically you don't make the same complaint three different times to three different entities and so I was more concerned about her safety than anything at that point."

After Ashley made her testimony, it made me feel relief that I had a good support system at my job. Ashley was very direct and did great. Next up would be Anthony's mom. She was sworn in, and Devra started direct examination with her. Devra asked her, "When was the last time you saw your granddaughter, Angelina?" She replied, "Angelina, I saw her for Thanksgiving of 2017." Devra asked, "And where did you see her?" She replied, "At my house." Devra inquired, "And how long was she at your house?" She said, "For a couple of days." Devra continued to ask her more questions like, "Who was there with her? And Prior to Thanksgiving 2017 when had you last seen your granddaughter?" Anthony's mom said, "When I had gone to Hungary in September, September 9th I believe." Devra confirmed with her that September 2017 was when she went to Hungary. Devra asked her, "And where did you see her in Hungary? Do you remember the town?" She looked down and said, "No, because everything is like, you know, a different language."

Between my lawyer, the judge and Pat they go around in circles on how his mom doesn't know what town her own son and granddaughter live in. The judge finds it very unusual that a mom doesn't know what town her son is living in.

Devra questioned Anthony's mom, "When you visited your granddaughter what language was, she primarily speaking when she was here, when she was here in November?" She answered, "She speaks mixed, both." It seems like we are going in complete circles again and his mom continues to stick her foot in her mouth. She says that she talks to Angelina every night on Skype. But when asked she also says that Angelina doesn't know English.

Devra continued with her questions and asked Anthony's mom, "A couple of years ago. Isn't it true that you took care of Angelina in August 2016 when Rebecca and Anthony went to the beach?" She said, "I don't remember them going to the beach." Devra asked about the trip Anthony, and I went to at Dewey Beach in August 2016. She said that she knew nothing about this trip that we took. Since I had phone records of when I called Anthony's mom Devra asked her if she remembered a phone call from me on September 4th, 2016. This was the phone conversation I had with her about how Anthony's friend told me that they took them into witness protection. She asked his mom if she remembered me calling and telling her that. Anthony's mom relied with a quick, "No." Last Devra asked her, "Did your son ever tell you he was in a witness protection program?" She replied, "He told me."

The judge asked to take a break from the questions and stated that she pulled up a map and that she is not familiar with the country of Hungary. She said that her point was that she is sharing with Anthony's mom that she has relatives who live in all kinds of foreign countries, and she might not be able to read the language, but she knows the name of the city where her children are going to be for foreign abroad semesters and even if they are only there for a month she studies where they will be. If her child or grandchild were living in a foreign county, she would at least be able to pronounce the name of the city. That is why she finds this so incredible that Anthony's mom doesn't know where her child is living. If she doesn't know the name of the elementary school, she is not that concerned but the town they are living in is of concern.

Devra asked her to bring along any communication that she would have had with her son, text messages, Facebook, emails, or pictures. Anthony's mom said that she only had pictures on her phone. She started fumbling with her phone and said that she does not know how to text message, which is not true. She could only find pictures that Anthony sent her and not any pictures that she took herself. She stated that she deleted everything. At one point the judge has her phone and is looking at pictures. More nonsense and wasted time happened with her playing dumb.

Almost the entire time the witnesses were examined the judge kept rolling her eyes and huffing and grunting because they were getting caught in their own lies. I made eye contact with her a few times, and she could see in my facial expressions that a lot of what was said was not true. His mom kept asking the judge if she could say more but she was denied. She was upset and walked out of the room to wait outside.

The last witness called into the room was Martin. He walked in and was as white as a sheet of paper. He appeared to be extremely nervous. Maybe he had something that he was hiding. Martin was sworn in, and Devra started asking him questions. She started with background information that he has been Anthony's business partner for years. They operated an entity that was a Real Estate Holding company.

Martin has some type of business still with Anthony based on his history and he knows where they are living but wouldn't tell the court. Plus, Anthony used Martin's mailing address on mortgage documents that he prepared and filed here in Dauphin County in August of 2015. Devra asked how Martin knew Anthony and he said that they met through a partnership that they were doing. She asked if it is an accurate statement that the two of them have been business partners in the past. Martin replied, "Yes."

His examination also continued to go in circles. Martin said he couldn't remember anything that Devra asked him. He can't remember when he last talked to Anthony. He is asked his age and if he has any memory problems or takes any medications affecting his memory. Martin keeps denying.

Devra asked Martin, "Did you speak to Rebecca around August of 2017?" He replied looking at me and said, "Is that when I met you at the Canal Street House?" I didn't answer his question. Devra asked, "So you would talk to Rebecca about Anthony from time to time. Is that right?" He said, "That time I did, yes." She asked him if he ever told me that he had learned that Anthony was in a witness protection program and Matin replied, "No." Devra asked Martin, "Did you ever tell Rebecca that Anthony had decided to move on with his life so she should move out?" His response was, "I didn't tell her to get out of the farmhouse. I told her to move on with her life."

The hearing began under a cloud of tension, the air thickened by the heated back-and-forth between the lawyers. Voices rose and fell, a cacophony of arguments and objections that seemed to reverberate off the courtroom walls. The judge, clearly eager to move things along, announced that she wanted to start with my friend Susie as the first witness.

Susie's testimony hinged on the photos she had taken at Saturday's Market, capturing Anthony, Ethel, and Angelina together. These images were irrefutable evidence of Anthony's deceit. Pat, Anthony's lawyer, surprisingly raised no objection to the photos and chose not to cross-examine Susie. It felt like a small victory, but the battle was far from over. Susie didn't even need to step into the courtroom; her pictures spoke volumes.

Next, Ashley was called to the stand for direct examination by Devra. As she answered routine questions about her employment and position, the tension in the room remained palpable.

"Did you have a meeting with Rebecca a couple of weeks ago regarding complaints you received about her?"

Pat immediately objected, questioning the relevance of any reports concerning my fitness as a registered nurse.

"If he had done that, I don't know how it's relevant to the custody proceedings." The judge, momentarily flustered, admitted she had nothing in front of her to reference.

Pat continued, revealing a picture of me in a noose, a grotesque attempt to question my mental stability. Devra seized the opportunity to highlight Anthony's retaliation tactics.

"Your Honor, the reporting of this to Penn State is relevant because it shows his efforts to retaliate against my client for anything she does to seek custodial rights for her child. He even discusses the custody case within this document, referencing a hearing that did not go as she expected."

Devra resumed questioning Ashley.

"When was that meeting? And what was the nature of this meeting?"

Ashley's response was reassuring.

"The nature of that meeting was to ensure Rebecca was in a safe place and to address any concerns about her safety." She confirmed that, despite Anthony's claims, there were no issues with my professional conduct or mental state.

Pat's cross-examination was a weak attempt to undermine Ashley's testimony. He asked about her role and the extent of her involvement. Ashley stood firm, confirming that her only concern had been my safety. She dismissed any issues with my professional conduct, validating my drug pulls and administration as appropriate.

Devra's follow-up questions to Ashley clarified the absurdity of Anthony's numerous complaints. Ashley explained that Anthony had made several redundant complaints within a short period, an unusual behavior that raised concerns more about his motives than my conduct. Each complaint seemed like a calculated move to destabilize me in the eyes of my employer and the court.

As Ashley's testimony concluded, I felt a wave of relief wash over me. Her clear, unwavering responses had fortified my position. But the battle was far from over. Anthony's mother was next, and her testimony promised to be another ordeal.

Anthony's mom was sworn in, and Devra began with straightforward questions about her last interactions with Angelina. Her answers were evasive and inconsistent. She couldn't even recall the town in Hungary where she claimed to have seen Angelina. The judge found it incredulous that a grandmother wouldn't know where her grandchild was living. Devra pressed on, highlighting the inconsistencies in her testimony. Anthony's mom claimed to speak to Angelina every night on Skype, yet also stated that Angelina didn't know English. Her contradictions painted a picture of confusion and deceit. Then, Devra struck a critical blow. She asked Anthony's mom if she remembered a phone call from me on September 4, 2016, about Anthony's supposed involvement in a witness protection program. Anthony's mom's quick denial was suspiciously defensive.

The judge's patience was wearing thin. She remarked on the improbability of a grandmother not knowing the town where her grandchild lived, underscoring the absurdity of Anthony's mom's claims. The judge's skepticism was palpable, and it felt like a silent acknowledgment of the truth I had been fighting to prove. Anthony's mom fumbled with her phone, unable to produce any meaningful evidence. She claimed to have deleted everything, further straining her credibility. The judge's exasperation was clear, her eyes rolling and sighs audible as Anthony's mom's testimony crumbled under scrutiny.

Finally, Martin was called to the stand. His demeanor was markedly different; he appeared pale and nervous, as if concealing a dark secret. Devra began by establishing his long-standing business relationship with Anthony. Martin's evasiveness was frustrating. He claimed not to remember crucial details and denied having any memory problems or taking medications that could affect his recall.

Devra's questioning revealed Martin's reluctance to disclose any information that could incriminate Anthony. He admitted to meeting me at the Canal Street House but denied ever telling me that Anthony was in a witness protection program. His contradictions were glaring, and his nervousness only added to the sense that he was hiding something. As Devra pressed further, it became clear that Martin was trying to protect Anthony. He admitted to telling me to "move on with my life," a statement that carried a heavy implication. His evasiveness and selective memory painted a picture of a man caught between loyalty and the truth.

The judge called for a break, her frustration evident. She shared her incredulity at Anthony's mom's ignorance of her son's and granddaughter's whereabouts, likening it to a parent not knowing the city where their child was studying abroad. Her analogy underscored the implausibility of the testimonies given by Anthony's family.

As the hearing continued, the judge's skepticism grew. She questioned the validity of the evidence and the credibility of the witnesses on Anthony's side. Each lie and contradiction brought me closer to revealing the truth. The courtroom drama was a relentless battle of wills, a fight for justice and the truth. As the witnesses were examined, the judge's exasperation mirrored my own frustration. Her skeptical glances and sighs were small, silent affirmations of the inconsistencies and deceit we were uncovering.

In the end, it was a grueling process, but each witness's testimony chipped away at the facade Anthony had built. The judge's growing skepticism and the relentless pursuit of the truth by Devra and my supporters provided a glimmer of hope in this arduous journey. I held onto that hope, knowing that the truth would ultimately prevail.

The moment had arrived for my cross-examination by Pat. Despite the high stakes, I felt a surprising wave of confidence and calm wash over me. The hours of preparation with Devra had fortified my resolve. She had drilled into me the importance of keeping my answers succinct—"yes" or "no"—to avoid giving Pat any ammunition to twist my words against me. Pat wasted no time diving into the most sensitive topics.

"Have you ever wanted to kill yourself? Have you taken drugs?" he asked, his tone sharp and probing.

"Yes," I replied steadily. "I have a prescription for Ativan to help me sleep."

The judge intervened almost immediately.

"This is not relevant," she declared, stopping Pat in his tracks. He erupted in outrage, but the judge remained firm, shutting down his line of questioning. My cross-examination was over as abruptly as it had begun, and I felt a rush of relief. All those hours of practice had paid off, and Pat's attempt to undermine me had been thwarted.

The hearing had already dragged on for hours, and the courthouse was nearing closing time. Devra began to cross-examine Anthony via Skype, but he seemed determined to derail the process. Every question prompted him to elaborate unnecessarily, forcing the judge to repeatedly remind him to keep his answers brief and to the point.

At one particularly frustrating juncture, the judge had to raise her voice, instructing Pat to control his client. Anthony's evasiveness about his home address was infuriating. He had used an address in Hungary on court documents, but it turned out to be Ethel's grandmother's house, not their current residence. The judge's patience was wearing thin, and it showed.

Pat had to step out multiple times to calm Anthony down. As the courthouse closing time loomed, the judge asked Anthony if I could speak to my daughter on the phone. His answer was a swift, unyielding "no." We then requested to Skype with Angelina in the courtroom, but again, Anthony refused. The judge's frustration boiled over.

"When this does go to an actual child custody hearing, this is going to look bad for you," she shouted into the computer screen before storming out of the room, bringing the hearing to an abrupt end.

With no resolution in sight, another hearing had to be scheduled. I walked out, exhausted and emotionally drained. A police officer who had been waiting outside recognized me from a previous protection from abuse court hearing and commented on the complexity of my case. His words hit me hard, making me feel sick to my stomach. *Was my situation really that dire?*

Devra emerged from the conference room looking equally worn out but offered some words of encouragement.

"You did good," she said, her exhaustion evident.

The constant battle with Pat had taken its toll on both of us. Anthony's refusal to let me communicate with Angelina was a harsh reminder of his manipulative nature. He had told me once that he wouldn't lose Angelina like he lost his son from his first marriage, a chilling declaration that now seemed more sinister than ever.

Throughout the hearing, I had presented irrefutable evidence: photos of Anthony and me at the beach in Delaware dated August 2016, proof of cash payments on the home equity loan in Pennsylvania, and a picture of Angelina from August 1, 2016—the last time I saw her. I also had records from an auto insurance claim Anthony had made in the United States during the time he claimed to be in Hungary. His photocopies of his passport were blurry and unconvincing, and he admitted to forgetting his trips in and out of the country. His narrative of me being a danger to him and Angelina was falling apart under the weight of evidence.

Anthony's attempts to paint me as mentally unstable were transparent. I had hundreds of text messages proving that he had been in communication with me, claiming we were still together. His story kept shifting, and he even showed the court recent pictures of himself with Angelina, Ethel, and their new baby, clearly staged for the hearing. Despite everything, Angelina's radiant smile in those photos gave me a glimmer of hope.

On our drive back, my parents told me that Anthony's mom had been playing videos of Angelina singing on her phone, despite claiming she didn't know how to text or send pictures. Her behavior was vindictive, a cruel attempt to hurt my parents. She had always portrayed herself as a devout Christian, but her actions revealed a different story. Once home, I changed into comfortable clothes, trying to shake off the day's emotional weight. Devra emailed me later, confirming that the judge had no concerns about my mental health, dismantling Anthony's primary defense. Now, we just had to wait for the next hearing.

The following day, Anthony had two of his friends write letters to the judge, claiming his mom was disoriented and needed help at the airport during her trip to Hungary. The judge dismissed these letters, seeing through the feeble attempt to cover up her lies. Anthony's mom's testimony had been a disaster, only making their case look more ridiculous. Devra stressed the importance of getting legal counsel in Hungary, and we reached out to a lawyer in New York City for assistance. The costs were staggering, and I had to take out a loan on my retirement savings. It felt like a financial black hole, but I trusted Devra's judgment.

March 29, 2018, marked the second part of the hearing. My parents, Katie, and Susie were there again, waiting outside on the wooden benches. Devra and I took our seats in the conference room, and the judge entered. We all stood up as the hearing began. Anthony appeared via video conference once more. Devra resumed her cross-examination, focusing on the discrepancies in his addresses and his income from selling his restaurant. When asked about paying taxes, Anthony casually admitted he didn't, shocking the judge.

The questioning continued, with Devra pressing Anthony on various dates and communications. He became increasingly agitated, and the judge had to intervene to stop his ranting. Anthony presented a self-made chart of his passport pages, which were missing and blurry. His credibility was crumbling. Anthony's attempts to recall the petition for modification dates were convoluted, and he name-dropped one of his criminal lawyers. His responses were a chaotic mix of dates and irrelevant details, making it clear he was trying to obfuscate the truth. Devra asked about the text messages and emails between us. Anthony claimed memory issues from a stroke, denying the authenticity of the emails.

"Sir, you were not asked if you remember them," the judge clarified. "You were asked if these are true and correct copies of emails between you and Rebecca."

Anthony eventually admitted they were.

Devra's final question to Anthony was whether he had allowed me any communication with Angelina. His answer was a definitive "no," despite my daily requests. With no further questions, Pat began his redirect examination.

Pat leaned forward, eyes narrowing as he addressed Anthony.

"Anthony, I have a couple of follow-ups. One of the earlier questions was whether you had told Rebecca you were in a witness protection program. You had explained what occurred. Why would you—and I think at the end of the day you allowed Rebecca to believe you were in a witness protection program. Why would you have allowed her to believe that?"

qAnthony inhaled deeply, his voice tinged with a mixture of frustration and sorrow.

"Because this girl, two times she tried to kill me. She tried to harm her own daughter. Before I took custody of my daughter, she would lock her in the room, and my daughter would tell me. Then after, when I did take custody, I came to visit Rebecca at the farmhouse. And when I went to leave with my wife, Ethel—because my wife, Ethel, came—we all went to leave. Rebecca was mad and Angelina actually—we left because Rebecca got mad, and Angelina did not want to give her a kiss goodbye. So, Rebecca turned away. When she opened the door and Angelina turned around and went to walk out, Rebecca turned away and called her own daughter a name. At that time, we had no more visits. That was it. We went to once a month. Once every two months. That's it."

Pat, relentless in his pursuit, continued.

"So, my question was why would you allow her to believe you were in the witness protection program? I believe that your testimony so far is 'she tried to kill me twice. She tried to harm our daughter.' Were there any other reasons?"

Anthony's eyes flared with a mix of anger and desperation.

"Yeah. To protect my wife. My wife that I have now. So, she did not know where I was. She gave up custody of the kid. She had no more rights to do—no more than a stranger. She gave up custody, physical, everything. She has no more rights. The other reason was because I knew she was lying to me. She was saying she wanted to get back. She wanted to get back. That was all a lie. She was waiting. It was a lie. There's documentation. There are emails, text messages, all that. She's been dating another guy and this and that. So, I was lying to her like she was lying to me. She was sending me naked pictures, videos to me. I have all this stuff. We presented it."

Anthony's words felt like sharp daggers, each one more painful than the last. His defense mechanism of projection was in full swing, accusing me of infidelities to deflect from his own deceit. My frustration simmered beneath the surface, a cauldron of anger and resignation. I wasn't surprised; I had braced myself for this onslaught of lies. Yet, hearing him twist our past so cruelly stung. All I could think was wow, but I wasn't surprised with all of Anthony's lies and how he took one incident that happened and twisted it. I had no idea I was even divorced, and that he had married Ethel.

The conversation veered into the absurd as Pat and Anthony discussed my new car, painting me as extravagant despite my bankruptcy. The truth was far simpler—my parents had helped me get a used car after I left Anthony, and I managed the affordable monthly payments. But the narrative his lawyer spun was far more sinister.

Devra began to cross-examine Anthony.

"You allowed Rebecca to believe that you were in a witness protection program to protect your wife, right?"

Anthony, visibly agitated, replied.

"I allowed her—yes. I allowed her to believe that to protect my wife and child and myself also."

Devra pressed on.

"You wanted to get back together with Rebecca as well. Correct?"

Anthony's voice wavered, a hint of defensiveness crept in.

"This is 2014: she was pursuing me. Before the divorce in 2014, when she filed for her first divorce, I said she wanted to get back together with me. That's when I –I went and talked to my friend Terry, and I said, Terry, what do you think I should do? He said Anthony, talk to God. I went to church. I called Terry. Me and Terry had a long, long talk. And every time I had told him who—he said, call me. I called him, and he was right there for me the whole time. Until it became dangerous, then I said, okay, you know what? I gave it a try. At that time, she tried to kill me. She hired that girl. And Terry asked, well, what did you do wrong Anthony. And I said, well, maybe I cheated on her, He said, well, that's going to make her mad. And that's what happened. So, if you did something wrong, you know what? Now it's 2014. So, I gave her another chance. She tried to kill me. She hired a girl, and her boyfriend came over with a gun, waved it around in the room, and she waited there three hours with the girl. Her excuse, up until this day, is I just wanted to know you were cheating on me, Anthony, I wasn't going to kill you."

Devra remained composed; her voice unwavering.

"Okay. So, you are alleging that in 2013, 2014 that Rebecca did all these horrible things, threatened you, tried to have you killed, all these kinds of things, is that right?"

"Yes."

Devra's eyes bore into him.

"Yet you continued to have sexual relations with her and continued an intimate relationship with her up until at least November 2017. Is that right?"

Anthony's voice grew defensive.

"No. I divorced her in 2015. I gave her—"

But Devra cut him off, pressing the point.

"And you continued to have sex with her?"

Anthony stammered.

"I explained it to you just now. I gave her a second chance."

Devra's voice was sharp, cutting through the courtroom tension.

"You're claiming that she's such a threat and so dangerous, yet you consistently asked her to send you videos and messages a private—"

Pat stood up, his voice booming across the room.

"Objection. Relevance. Just because someone is dangerous doesn't mean that you're not sexually attracted to them. Just for example, I'm not admitting anything, but how is this relevant?"

Anthony's stories were a tangled web of lies, each more outlandish than the last. Devra called me back as a witness for direct examination. She asked about the messages between Anthony and me, verifying their authenticity. The judge intervened, questioning Pat about the frequency and nature of communication between me and my daughter.

Pat's response was slippery.

"Anthony is concerned that the communication with the mother at this point would be detrimental to his daughter, and he's indicating that he doesn't believe that it's in her best interest for that to occur."

The judge's tone was stern, addressing Anthony directly.

"Sir, you do understand that this will be used against you at any custody hearing, whether it's here or Hungary?"

Anthony's reply was defiant.

"I understand. They didn't file for custody until they found out that I was married with a kid."

The judge's response was swift and unyielding.

"No, sir. It has nothing to do with that. It has to do with alienating the child from her mother, regardless of who has physical or legal custody. I just want you to be sure that you understand that this will be used against you no matter what judge hears this custody trial. Because this is very bad behavior on your part."

The hearing felt like a never-ending loop, a grim parody of justice. The lawyers' voices rose and fell in heated arguments, the tension palpable. Pat had to leave the room several times to calm Anthony down. At one point, I saw Pat's frustration reach a boiling point, his eyes rolling upwards in exasperation, shaking his head. Anthony's attempts to shout objections without the authority to do so showcased his narcissistic tendencies in full display. If the judge could see through the facade and recognize the duress I was under when Anthony tricked me into signing those papers in 2015, I might have a chance at winning jurisdiction.

After the hearing concluded, a heavy wave of exhaustion washed over me. My emotions were frayed, and all I yearned for was the sanctuary of home, a place where I could let my guard down and rest. But as soon as I walked through the door, my phone buzzed with a series of urgent emails from Devra. She needed certain papers written up for the Hungarian lawyers immediately. Despite my fatigue, I dove into the task with a sense of urgency. My life had become a relentless cycle of working my real job and gathering every scrap of information that could help our case. Every time Devra needed documents or specific information, I responded without delay, determined not to let anything slip through the cracks.

We began corresponding with a lawyer in Hungary, a beacon of hope in this convoluted mess. She meticulously reviewed everything Devra had sent. But then came the crushing blow—after her research, she informed us that she couldn't practice in the court where Anthony lived. My heart sank, a deep sense of disappointment gnawing at me. It felt like another financial drain, another dead end.

Desperate, Devra reached out to the lawyer in New York City again, who then referred us to another attorney. The cycle of paperwork resumed, each form filled and email sent a small act of defiance against the mounting despair.

The new Hungarian lawyer insisted on communicating everything through me. One email, stark and final, declared it was too late to challenge Anthony. My stomach churned as I read his words. I had never officially received the Hungarian court papers; everything felt like it was slipping through my fingers. He said I would have to travel to Hungary and appear in court in person, a daunting prospect given my financial constraints.

The reality hit me hard—there was no feasible way I could afford to make that trip. The sense of helplessness was overwhelming, a crushing weight on my already burdened shoulders. Despite all my efforts, the path forward seemed more uncertain than ever.

··· Chapter Fourteen

I was nestled in the family room, cocooned in a blanket on the recliner, trying to unwind after a hectic day at work. The television murmured in the background, but my mind was a whirlwind of thoughts. An uneasy feeling prompted me to check my bank account. Logging into the banking website, I felt my heart thud as I saw my checking account balance dwindling down to the last couple of thousand dollars. Panic gripped me. *How had I burned through my retirement funds so quickly?* The loan I took out against my retirement was substantial, yet here I was, almost broke. My chest tightened, and a wave of anxiety crashed over me.

I had to figure out a financial plan quickly. My family wasn't wealthy. Both of my parents were retired, and I couldn't bear the thought of taking their hard-earned retirement money. They, along with my grandmother, had already given me so much, and guilt gnawed at me every time I accepted their help. The hearing on jurisdiction had ended, but the judge hadn't made any decisions yet. There were no agreements allowing me to talk to my daughter, which left me feeling utterly defeated. My thoughts were consumed with finding a way to see her, and the stress was relentless.

The email from the Hungarian lawyer was the final blow. He laid out a series of pros and cons, expressing concerns that Hungary might indeed have jurisdiction. His questions and suggestions felt like a labyrinth with no clear way out. Each option seemed fraught with potential pitfalls and heartache. The idea of physically going to Hungary, dealing with court proceedings there, and facing Anthony's possible retaliation was overwhelming. I couldn't afford the travel, nor did I have the emotional strength to face him.

Crushed by the weight of it all, I retreated to my room and broke down in tears. I no longer had the funds to retain Devra, and the prospect of continuing the fight seemed impossible. The fear of Anthony hurting me, or having others do so, was ever-present, casting a dark shadow over my every thought. I felt a profound sadness and defeat, sapping my desire to go to the gym or even talk about the situation with friends and coworkers. When they asked how things were going, I would just say I was waiting for news. Talking about it felt like reliving the nightmare.

After much soul-searching, I decided to tell Devra that I couldn't go through with retaining Hungarian counsel. My dwindling funds needed to be spent wisely, and my focus had to shift to bringing my daughter back to the United States. Angelina was a US citizen, and she belonged here with me. The harsh reality that I might not see her again until she turned eighteen began to sink in. If she ever looked for me, at least she would know I tried my hardest to get her back.

Some mornings, as I sat in my car before work, I'd scroll through Facebook and see memories of Angelina—pictures of her as a baby or a few years old. The images of us smiling together hit me like a punch to the gut, leaving me breathless and struggling to compose myself before heading into work. The emotional toll was profound, making me moodier and more sluggish. My eating habits deteriorated, and my days became a blur of work and fitful sleep.

One Saturday morning, a text from Amanda, my high school friend, offered a glimmer of hope. She asked how I was doing, and I realized it might be nice to reconnect. Amanda had always made me laugh until my stomach hurt. Though Anthony had tried to isolate me from her, she had always tried to check in on me. We arranged to hang out, and as soon as we started talking, it was like no time had passed. We fell back into our old rhythm, joking and sharing stories.

Amanda confessed she was also going through a tough time, having just ended a long-term relationship and starting a new job. She said seeing me motivated her to get moving again. We decided to go out that night, meeting up with friends and hitting a few bars. For the first time in ages, I felt a flicker of my old self. I realized that I wasn't the ugly, useless person Anthony had made me believe I was. I saw the beautiful person I had always been, hidden beneath layers of his manipulation and control.

Amanda had tried to get me to leave Anthony countless times. But leaving a relationship like that is a decision only you can make, and it often takes a long time to gather the strength. I'm grateful I made it out alive because some women don't. Escaping from a dangerous relationship requires careful planning and immense courage. That night with Amanda reminded me of my worth and the life I could reclaim, one step at a time.

That night when Amanda and I went out, an unexpected twist of fate led me to meet someone new. He asked me out on a date, and though I was a bundle of nerves, I decided to give it a try. At that point, my fear threshold had been stretched to its limits; nothing could make me more anxious than I already was. We went on a few dates, and he turned out to be a nice guy with a stable career in information technology. But as kind as he was, he was also incredibly dull. Amanda kept reminding me to be grateful that he wasn't a jerk or mean, and she was right. Yet, I knew deep down he wasn't what I was looking for.

Reintegrating into a normal life felt like stepping into an alien world. For over a year, my existence had been confined to waiting for my daughter to come home, cloistered in my house, cut off from the outside world. Anthony's lies had kept me in a perpetual state of limbo, always promising, "Just one more month and we will be home." That day never arrived. The clarity with which I now saw his mistreatment filled me with a simmering rage. Sharing my story with close friends and seeing their horrified reactions was both validating and terrifying. It underscored just how wrong his behavior had been and confirmed that I was right to free myself from that toxic life.

Returning home felt like a bittersweet failure. On one hand, it was the best decision for my healing and learning to live again. On the other, it felt like admitting defeat. Loneliness had frayed my mental state; I had depended solely on Anthony. I felt like I was failing because I didn't have Angelina or the family I had envisioned. During those solitary days, I lived in constant fear that missing a mortgage payment would provoke Anthony to harm me in the middle of the night. But without those fears, I began to feel a newfound sense of peace. I started to relax and breathe for the first time since I was seventeen, before I met Anthony.

Living at home with my brother was comforting. My sister, though married and living an hour away, was also a source of support. The longer commute to work was a small price to pay for the stability I found in a reliable car and a loving family. Gradually, I began to feel happier. My mood lightened as I adjusted to the rhythms of a normal life—spending holidays with family, celebrating milestones, and simply being present. I cherished moments with my niece, moments I would never have had if I were still with Anthony.

The aftermath of my abusive relationship left me grappling with feelings of inadequacy, convinced I was unlovable and somehow deserving of the abuse. I blamed myself for losing Angelina. But I knew I had to rebuild my self-esteem. I had to be kinder to myself, to stop the relentless self-criticism. It was a challenge to learn to say "no" without guilt or to stop apologizing incessantly. Each day was a struggle to embrace positive thoughts, to tell myself, "I deserve this life." My self-esteem began to heal through the love and support of my family, friends, and coworkers. They helped me balance the negative shadows of my past, reminding me that I deserved love and respect.

Anthony had isolated me from my family, monitoring my conversations and controlling my visits. His fear that they would encourage me to leave him had kept me in a state of near captivity. Nearly two years of my life were wasted waiting for Angelina, believing his promises, and enduring his lies. Keeping my daughter from me was one of the cruelest things he could have done.

As I awaited the judge's decision on jurisdiction, Devra reassured me that the judge was on my side and would do everything possible to keep the case in the United States. But the wait was agonizing.

That April, Angelina turned six. It was the second birthday I missed, and the pain was unbearable. I cried that morning before work, haunted by thoughts of her—wondering if she was happy, if she felt loved. That day at work, my clinical manager approached me, tears in her eyes, to tell me I had been reported to the Department of State. I assured her I would cooperate fully. Just days after Angelina's birthday, I found myself in a meeting with a state investigator, a state trooper, and a human resources officer. Anthony had filed a complaint against me, but I was determined to show him that I couldn't be broken.

The meeting was brief, and I was required to undergo a psychiatric evaluation to close the case. Mother's Day came and went, another bitter reminder of what I had lost. I was losing hope, teetering on the edge of giving up. In a moment of desperation, I called Amanda, hoping for some semblance of joy. She suggested I meet a friend of hers, someone she thought would be perfect for me.

On a Friday night, I went to Amanda's house after work. Her friend, Kevin, a mechanic, was supposed to join us. As the night dragged on, I was ready to give up until he finally arrived. He walked in, barely acknowledging me, and continued chatting with Amanda. We decided to grab pizza next door, and as we sat down, Kevin began to open up. Though he dominated the conversation, I found myself intrigued. Amanda discreetly signaled for my opinion, and I gave her a thumbs down, thinking he wasn't interested in me.

Back at Amanda's house, we decided to visit a local club for a laugh. While Amanda smoked outside, Kevin and I waited in her kitchen. He started talking about dogs, and right then, I decided I liked him. At the club, he asked me to pretend to be his girlfriend, and we began to talk more deeply. I shared my complicated custody battle, unsure if he would believe me or be scared off. But he remained interested. The club was outdated and eerie, but we had fun. Back at Amanda's house, we watched a movie, and I was startled by her pet lizard, instinctively jumping into Kevin's arms. We all went to bed, and Kevin stayed over since he had been drinking. That night, he kissed me, and it felt amazing. He held me all night, and for the first time in years, I felt safe. The following morning, he kissed me again before leaving for work, and I felt a strange sense of comfort with him.

Kevin and I continued to see each other, and he quickly became a significant part of my life. I was nervous, but he made me feel comfortable. We spent weekends together, and he introduced me to his family. Kevin had his own struggles, having recently lost his brother in a car accident. We supported each other, and I felt a happiness I had never known.

June flew by without any word from the judge. One day at work, I received a call from security, informing me that the FBI was waiting to speak with me. My friend Katie and I waited nervously. The FBI agent, accompanied by hospital security and a state trooper, explained that Anthony had filed a complaint. They asked if I wanted to harm my ex-husband. Though I could have jokingly said "yes," I firmly told them "no." They apologized and advised me to be careful.

The encounter left me puzzled, but Katie sensed there might be more to it. Anthony's harassment continued, but I was stronger now. By July and August, Kevin and I were inseparable, even taking trips to the beach. He asked why I never got angry, and I smiled, unable to explain. He treated me with kindness and respect, something I was still learning to accept. His patience and understanding began to heal the wounds left by my abusive past. I was learning what a healthy relationship felt like—feeling safe, wanted, and loved. It was a revelation after years of abuse. Anthony had trained me to fear conflict, but with Kevin, I was beginning to unlearn those reactions. I vowed to embrace this new chapter, cherishing the love and support I had found.

As I navigated this new relationship, I realized that good people do exist. I was finally experiencing the joy and security I deserved, and it was a powerful reminder that even in the darkest times, there was hope for a brighter future.

··· Chapter Fifteen

On a Wednesday afternoon in August, I found myself enveloped in the familiar chaos of the hospital's radiology unit. The procedure suite was bustling, and I was fully immersed in sedating a patient for a biopsy. My day had been relentless, starting with back-to-back procedures from eight in the morning. The heavy lead apron I wore in the CT scan room weighed me down, both physically and mentally. Exhausted and yearning for the solace of a hot shower, I counted the hours until I could clock out. My evening plans were simple yet rejuvenating: a visit to the nail salon and packing for another blissful weekend at the beach with Kevin.

Between cases, I noticed a missed call from an unfamiliar number. I brushed it off, thinking it could wait, but a few minutes later, a text message flashed on my screen.

"Rebecca, can you call me regarding papers I need to give you. I don't want to come to you because I'm in uniform. I am in temporary parking out front. Thanks, Constable."

A sense of dread washed over me. Stepping outside the procedure suite, I informed my nurse manager and sought Katie's opinion. We both suspected it was another one of Anthony's schemes, likely Hungarian court papers or child support documents.

I tried to push the unsettling thoughts aside as I prepared for the next biopsy. I was flustered but focused on my patient. Meanwhile, the constable had made his way down to the radiology unit. Katie, ever the fierce protector, confronted him with the hospital's security team. Their presence was a stark reminder that my workplace was a sanctuary where I should not be ambushed. After some tense moments, the constable left. Katie, ever the loyal friend, accompanied me to my car, ensuring I was safe.

Determined not to let Anthony's tactics ruin my day, I proceeded to the nail salon and then headed to Kevin's place. With him, I felt an unshakeable sense of security. Later, I learned that the constable had indeed served my parents with Hungarian papers while they were relaxing on their deck. Anthony had orchestrated this, but his efforts were futile.

The papers declared that Hungary had jurisdiction—a fact we already knew. Anthony had business dealings that required frequent travel between Hungary and the US. Despite his attempts to sever ties, he remained a US citizen with properties and assets here. Katie suggested I consult a Hungarian doctor we worked with. He translated the documents, revealing that the property Anthony claimed was merely a modest cabin on a small plot of land, worth no more than fifty thousand dollars.

I sent the documents to Devra, my attorney, who confirmed they were identical to those received in April. Participating in the Hungarian court system was not an option; the financial burden of travel and legal fees was insurmountable. Katie's curiosity led her to Google the address listed on the papers. It turned out to be a resort in Hungary, complete with vacation cabins, a white pony, swimming pools, and a banquet hall. Anthony had turned this place into a hideaway for his new family, using Hungary to spite me and deny me access to my daughter.

That Friday, Devra contacted me with news that Anthony had

requested to terminate his relationship with his attorney due to billing disputes. The judge approved, leaving Anthony without legal representation. It was a small victory in a week fraught with tension.

Kevin and I escaped to the beach for the weekend, a much-needed respite from the stress. The ocean's embrace, delicious food, and Kevin's infectious laughter made time fly. By Monday morning, I was back home, savoring the extended break from work. After unpacking and taking a nap, I checked the county docket pages online. My heart raced as I read the new orders.

"Upon consideration of (1) Plaintiffs Preliminary Objections to Defendants Petition for Modification of Custody Order and Petition for Special Relief and (2) Plaintiffs Motion to Transfer Venue and following two days of hearings and receipt of post hearing briefs it is hereby directed that Plaintiffs Preliminary Objection contesting Pennsylvania jurisdiction is OVERRULED and the Motion to Transfer Venue to Hungary is DENIED. It is further directed that a conciliation on Defendants Petition for Modification of Custody shall be scheduled. See Complete Order, filed. Copies distributed by Chambers 08/17/2018."

Tears of joy streamed down my face. The US retained jurisdiction! I rushed downstairs to share the incredible news with my parents. There was hope—a tangible, beautiful hope. Moments later, Devra called and I could barely contain my elation as I told her I'd read the dockets. We had won jurisdiction. The battle was far from over, but this victory was a beacon of light in my darkest days.

When Anthony had a lawyer, he confidently declared that even if I won jurisdiction, he would appeal it. His words echoed in my mind as I dialed each number, sharing the joyous news with friends and family. Devra had sent me the official order, and I could almost feel the fire of Anthony's anger and frustration from miles away. I hoped he felt a pang of defeat, a taste of the turmoil he had forced upon me. My heart swelled with hope and happiness, emotions that had been strangers to me for so long. For the first time in ages, a genuine smile graced my face. I was gaining weight healthily, eating full meals, and discovering that life held more than the shadows of an abusive relationship.

Despite this newfound happiness, I remained vigilant. The scars of my past made me cautious, always looking over my shoulder. I carried protection, ready to defend myself if needed. My visits to my grandma's for target practice were both a precaution and a form of empowerment. I had left my abusive relationship with a firm resolution to avoid romantic entanglements for fear of falling into another harmful situation. Trust was a fragile thing, and rebuilding it seemed daunting.

Counseling and a strong support system, especially my friend Amanda, played crucial roles in my recovery. They showed me it was okay to meet new people, to open up again. Gradually, I learned to trust Kevin, identifying and managing my triggers. PTSD, anxiety, and depression lingered, but I was learning to navigate them. Certain smells, sounds, and even music could trigger me, but I was developing coping mechanisms. Trust was the cornerstone of my relationship with Kevin, and sharing my story with him was both terrifying and liberating.

Anthony was used to winning, and I wouldn't have been surprised if he resorted to physical harm. My awareness of my surroundings became almost second nature. I scanned every room for exits and scrutinized the crowd, knowing I could never afford to be oblivious again.

One Friday evening in September, after a workout at the gym, I decided to treat myself to some shopping at the outlets in Hershey. I bought new jeans and tank tops, envisioning a fun night out with Kevin. The victory of winning jurisdiction lifted a significant weight off my shoulders, bringing me a step closer to my daughter. As I sat on a bench outside the stores, enjoying the cool fall breeze and catching up on emails, an unexpected message from Devra appeared. Anthony had hired another lawyer, located two hours away, and was filing an appeal against the judge's order of jurisdiction. My stomach churned, and nausea hit me like a wave. An appeal could drag on for years and drain resources I didn't have. I called my friend Pam, seeking solace in her unwavering reassurance that Anthony was merely a coward trying to delay the inevitable.

Breaking the news to my mom was equally gut-wrenching. We had anticipated this move, but the reality was still a bitter pill to swallow. That night, Kevin and I went out with friends. His presence was a balm to my frayed nerves, a reminder that I wasn't alone in this fight.

A few days later, I had a conference call with Devra. She informed me that Anthony's attorney had filed the appeal two days late. We decided to wait and see if the superior court would dismiss the appeal due to the late filing. Anthony's lawyer had submitted a motion citing a medical illness as the cause for the delay, but it was a flimsy excuse.

By October, Devra sent me the order from the superior court that the appeal was denied. Relief washed over me, and tears of joy followed. The lengthy, costly appeal process had been averted. My family and friends rejoiced with me.

As the child custody conference in November approached, I was a bundle of nerves. I had no idea if Anthony would show up, but his lawyer indicated that the date worked for him. His absence would only further tarnish his image.

At that time, an intense wave of fatigue and nausea hit me. It was different from anything I'd felt before. My friend Katie noticed and handed me a pregnancy test. I hurried to the bathroom near the nurse's station, and within moments, a strong line confirmed it: I was pregnant! Joy erupted from Katie as she handed me orange juice and insisted I get prenatal vitamins immediately.

With only an hour left in my shift, I called Kevin. His voice was tired, but he agreed to meet for dinner. I wanted to tell him in person. Nervously, I drove to the car dealership where he worked. As we sat in my car, I blurted out, "I'm pregnant!" His initial shock melted into happiness, and we decided to celebrate with wings at a nearby restaurant. His reaction was a world apart from Anthony's when I had told him about my first pregnancy.

This marked the beginning of a new chapter. My life was finally steering towards a positive direction. I was inching closer to regaining custody of my daughter, and I had a loving, supportive boyfriend in Kevin. My friends and family stood by me unwaveringly. People often asked how I remained so strong. The truth was, enduring Anthony's abuse had forged my resilience. I wouldn't rest until I held my daughter in my arms again. Strength was my only option, and I was prepared to fight for it every step of the way.

··· Chapter Sixteen

I spent countless long nights in my parents' kitchen, hunched over my laptop, surrounded by stacks of papers and empty coffee cups. The kitchen table became my makeshift war room, where I delved deep into the labyrinth of family law in Pennsylvania. Every night, I pored over legal texts, court cases, and procedural manuals, desperately searching for a way to bring Angelina home. My heart ached with each passing day, knowing that time was slipping through my fingers, making it harder to fight for her return, especially in Hungary, where Anthony's manipulations had already tilted the scales against me.

One evening, as I was lost in the sea of legal jargon, an email notification from Mickey popped up on my screen. My heart sank. I knew Mickey was struggling with everything that was happening. She wanted me to do more, but she couldn't understand the excruciating limitations I faced—the procedural hurdles, the financial constraints, the emotional toll. I realized, perhaps too late, that she was reliving her own traumatic past through my ordeal.

When I first met Mickey after starting to date Anthony, I noticed an unsettling dynamic between them. Their relationship was far from normal. Anthony's constant yelling and stern demeanor towards her were jarring. Weekends meant for father-daughter bonding turned into work shifts at the restaurant, where Mickey and I would toil away, only to return home without Anthony. My heart broke for her; a child deserved joy and time with her father, not to be pawned off to whoever he was dating at the time.

A few weeks before the custody conference, Mickey sent me an email that was both a lifeline and a harrowing glimpse into her past. She attached old court documents, including a psychiatric exam of Anthony, her personal account to the judge, and letters from Anthony's first wife detailing her abuse. Mickey's letter to the judge was a desperate plea for Angelina's safety. She revealed her chilling reality.

"Anthony is my biological father of twenty-four years. Angelina is one of my two half-siblings, and he has no relationship with the two eldest, myself and my brother. My brother has had no contact with Anthony since 2004 due to severe domestic violence involving his mother. My sister Angelina is the third child and the subject of this matter. In his current marriage, I also have another younger brother, whose name I do not know. He remarried a girl from Hungary less than a year after divorcing Rebecca."

Mickey's fear for Angelina was palpable. She had lived through the same nightmare and knew the patterns of Anthony's abuse all too well.

"Anthony attempted to buy my silence and 'love' throughout my childhood," she wrote. "He bought me horses, four-wheelers, dogs, and boat rides, only to take them away. I am certain he is doing the same with Angelina. She deserves a chance at a better life and healthier mental state, which Anthony or his family cannot provide."

Mickey's letter detailed the horrors of her childhood, including court-mandated visits that were frequently violated by Anthony. She recalled being dropped off at random women's houses for "supervised" visits, only to find Anthony there against court orders. Her life was a revolving door of courtrooms and traumatic experiences, with Anthony always looming like a dark cloud.

Her memories were a litany of abuse and terror. She recounted witnessing Anthony burn his first ex-wife's skin with a hairdryer, strangle her with the cord, and beat her within an inch of consciousness. She described the numerous women who had come and gone, all suffering under Anthony's brutality, and the animals he beat mercilessly.

> "If I even thought of helping or checking our pets, I would suffer the same," she wrote.

One incident stood out starkly in her mind. Her mother was once held in contempt of court for not producing Mickey in court for Anthony, who had threatened to take her out of the country.

> "Throughout my life, he threatened to take me to countries like Russia or Ukraine," she recalled. "I went into foster care at seventeen. The day before, he strangled me until I was almost unconscious and threatened to take me to Russia if I didn't end the CYS investigation."

Her mother had fought tirelessly to protect her, but it wasn't until a domestic violence incident involving the NJ SWAT team in 2003 that she managed to secure emergency relief of his rights to Mickey. Anthony was evaluated and noted as a possible Bipolar and Manic Sociopath. The abuse Mickey witnessed his ex-wife endure mirrored the experiences of countless other women, including myself. Mickey's plea to the judge was unequivocal.

"I do not recommend the paternal grandmother as any kind of guardian. She has enabled my father's abusive behavior. She hid the women he attacked, ignored court orders, and manipulated situations to protect him. I have minimized any connection to her, maintaining only minimal contact because of my great-grandmother, the only person on his side who ever defended me or my mother."

As I read Mickey's harrowing account, my resolve hardened. This wasn't just a legal battle; it was a fight for Angelina's very life and well-being. The weight of her words pressed down on me, but they also fueled my determination. I couldn't let Angelina suffer the same fate. I would navigate the labyrinth of family law, face every obstacle, and fight with every ounce of strength I had. For Angelina and for Mickey.

The email shattered me. Tears streamed down my face as I absorbed the raw pain and horror of her words. The torment she had witnessed and endured under Anthony's roof was almost too much to bear. A wave of nausea and anger surged through me. No child should ever have to experience such vile abuse. The thought that someone had seen my suffering firsthand as a child, and now echoed my own fears and traumas, left me feeling both sickened and enraged.

Mickey is a beacon of resilience. Today, she stands as a strong young woman, having found love and stability with a man who understands and respects her. Her smile is radiant, a testament to the freedom she has finally grasped after years of living under Anthony's shadow. Yet, like me, she remains vigilant, always looking over her shoulder, ready to protect herself from any future threats he might pose.

As I opened the next email attachment, a chilling psychological evaluation of Anthony unfolded before my eyes. The dates were seared into my memory: 5/7/04, 5/10/04, and 5/14/04, with the report finalized on 5/28/04. This was the same year I met Anthony, oblivious to the darkness that lay beneath his polished exterior. The judge had mandated this evaluation due to serious concerns raised during a court appearance related to parenting issues. Prior to this, Anthony had faced domestic violence charges, resulting in a restraining order that required him to undergo a risk assessment at his own expense. His future parenting time hinged on the results of this evaluation.

On May 7, 2004, Anthony arrived for the first appointment, looking immaculate in a suit and tie. He was cooperative, engaging in the testing activities with a veneer of charm. He even attempted to flirt with the psychologist, making inappropriate comments like, "You're a nice lady ... where did you get these questions? I guess I have to answer the questions that you tell me ... I'd hate to have your job ... you must see a lot of crazy people." The testing proceeded without incident, but his true nature simmered just beneath the surface.

By May 14, 2004, during the interview portion of the evaluation, Anthony maintained his polished appearance but revealed more of his manipulative traits. He spoke in a calm, modulated tone, attempting to portray himself as the victim while subtly discrediting his wife and ex-girlfriend. His responses were verbose, filled with unnecessary details aimed at self-aggrandizement. He intellectualized and name-dropped, trying to impress the psychologist. But when challenged, his patience snapped, and he made an abrupt, sarcastic comment, only to quickly apologize.

Anthony's recounting of his relationship with his wife painted a disturbing picture. He described her as an "Italian Princess" who cried to get her way, blaming their financial woes on her supposed greed. He claimed he had spoiled her with pianos and jewelry, only to be met with insatiable demands. He depicted their marriage as stable for two years until an accident halted his income, sparking her irrational jealousy. He recounted accusations from his wife about affairs with his secretary and an ex-girlfriend, who he claimed became his wife's lover—a situation he bizarrely accepted.

He detailed opening a restaurant in Harrisburg, PA, despite his wife's disapproval, and subsequent jealousy over his female staff. His narrative shifted to accusations against his wife, including a supposed setup that led to his wrongful arrest and a pending restraining order. He minimized his legal troubles, dismissing serious charges as mere "summary judgments" and providing distorted accounts of his criminal case management.

Anthony's self-portrayal was a twisted mix of denial and misplaced victimhood. He blamed his wife for the dissolution of their marriage, insisting he had been a good husband and still loved her, despite his derogatory remarks. His inability to accept responsibility for his actions and the distorted reality he presented were deeply disturbing. At the conclusion of the session, Anthony was asked about his son. His response was chillingly detached.

"It really has nothing to do with him ... the conflict from which all this stems, has nothing to do with him."

He then mentioned he had supervised visitation with his daughter, Mickey, every other Saturday at the YWCA in Pennsylvania, a statement that seemed to gloss over the gravity of his actions.

The psychological evaluation revealed much about Anthony's character. The results suggested that he minimized his responses and engaged in positive impression management. His high score on avoidance indicated a tendency to shy away from confrontation, never addressing issues, and thus carrying unresolved conflicts into new situations. This avoidance often led to sudden outbursts, resulting in verbally and physically aggressive behaviors—a dangerous cycle of repression and explosion.

An additional test Anthony completed was the House-Person-Tree test, a projective test designed to measure various aspects of personality. His drawings indicated deep-seated issues with feelings of inadequacy, which manifested as oppositional tendencies, hostility, and suspiciousness. Anthony's attempts to overcompensate for his sense of inferiority through a facade of superiority were evident. His need for strength and power, coupled with verbal aggressiveness and possible sadistic tendencies, painted a disturbing picture of a man struggling with his own demons.

Another test, the Thematic Apperception Test, revealed even more. This projective test, designed to uncover an individual's perception of interpersonal relationships, showed that Anthony's stories were "lacking in emotional content." He seemed incapable of genuine emotional connection, a hallmark of his narcissistic tendencies.

In summary, Anthony appeared to be a man deeply invested in presenting a "perfect picture" of his life, family, and marriage. He blamed his wife for shattering this illusion, casting himself as a victim of her jealousy and alleged "mafia connections." Throughout the interview, he frequently berated his wife for being materialistic, yet his own materialistic desires were just as evident. He accepted no responsibility for his role in the breakdown of their marriage, instead blaming others and manipulating situations to portray himself in a sympathetic light.

The evaluation concluded that Anthony's information was of questionable validity, given his tendencies to minimize, deny, and reframe accounts. He lacked empathy and insight into others' feelings, placing more value on his own and believing that others should defer to his wants and needs. This chilling portrait of Anthony made it clear what kind of person he truly was—a narcissist with a dangerous lack of self-awareness and a propensity for manipulation and control.

As I read through Anthony's psychological evaluation, everything clicked into place. I had studied these tests in nursing school, and I knew how foolproof they were. You couldn't cheat them; they exposed the truth lurking beneath the surface. The next few email attachments contained letters from Anthony's ex-wife, Carmela, each one a raw testament to the horrors she had endured.

Carmela's first letter was a desperate plea to her local court, detailing the violence she suffered at Anthony's hands. She was a 27-year-old mother of a 20-month-old son at the time, fighting Anthony in court for custody, child support, and alimony. Their marriage, which began on July

4, 2001, quickly descended into a nightmare of abuse. The most severe beating occurred on December 31, 2002. Anthony, after being absent for two weeks, erupted in rage when Carmela mentioned his girlfriend's name. He dragged her upstairs while she held their 6-month-old son, forcing her to drop the baby in his crib. For two agonizing hours, he beat her, resulting in a broken hand, cuts, bruises, a concussion, and wire marks around her neck from his attempts to strangle her. The horror didn't end there; he raped her on New Year's Day.

Carmela's story continued, recounting how Anthony took her and their baby to his mother's house in Ephrata, PA, to hide the evidence of his brutality. For two weeks, she received no medical attention. Anthony's control was absolute, his cruelty boundless.

In another letter, Carmela described an incident on October 18, 2003, which Anthony had once bragged about to me. She traveled to their restaurant in Harrisburg, PA, and found Anthony's girlfriend, Betty, working there. A fight ensued, and Anthony assaulted Carmela again. Fearing for her safety, she drove back to New Jersey, stopping at a police station for an escort. She packed her son's clothes and fled to her family's home, but Anthony's harassment continued. He showed up at her parents' house, causing scenes and trying to break in.

The police advised Carmela to obtain a restraining order, which she did. Anthony's response was a threat.

"You made the biggest mistake of your life by getting the police involved. I will shoot anyone who comes to the house."

This led to a tense standoff with SWAT teams and negotiators, ending with Anthony's arrest after twelve hours. The house was a fortress, with doors nailed shut, windows covered, and her son's video camera from his monitor hidden in the mailbox. The police confiscated eight thousand dollars from a safe in the car, revealing Anthony's deceit—he couldn't afford health insurance or proper child support, yet he had this hidden stash.

Carmela's letter was a desperate cry for help. She described living in constant fear, knowing Anthony's capacity for violence. His threats to kill her and their son were real, and the restraining order felt like a flimsy barrier against his wrath. Her words painted a picture of a life lived in terror, always looking over her shoulder, never feeling safe.

Reading Carmela's letters, I felt a deep connection to her pain. My own fourteen years with Anthony were a drawn-out horror, and her two years and three months of suffering mirrored my own experiences. Her bravery in documenting her ordeal and reaching out for help was a testament to her strength. Her story was a stark reminder of the evil lurking within Anthony, a man who thrived on control and instilled fear in those around him. It was like staring into a mirror reflecting my own past—an agonizing reminder of the torment I had endured. Each plea for help tugged at my heartstrings, filling me with a profound sadness. In many ways, Carmela and I were kindred spirits, both victims of a monstrous man. She came from a loving, normal family, untouched by abuse or violence, and understood what it meant to genuinely love and be loved. The physical, mental, and sexual abuse, inflicted by the same cruel hands that once tormented me, were eerily identical to my own experiences with Anthony.

There was a chilling pattern to his abuse, a methodical cruelty that revealed his calculated nature. While Carmela's suffering began immediately upon marrying him, Anthony had taken a different approach with me. He groomed me meticulously in the first few months, presenting a facade of charm and care before revealing his true, abusive self. It was as if he had learned from his past mistakes, refining his methods to ensure a tighter grip on me. I was only eighteen when I met him, young and impressionable, making it easier for him to ensnare me in his web of control.

But his threats extended beyond the abuse. With both Carmela and his first ex-wife, he wielded the menace of taking them out of the country as a weapon of terror. But with me, it wasn't just a threat—he took my daughter out of the country, a violation so profound it left scars on my soul.

With this new information, the fight for Angelina's safety took on a renewed urgency. I couldn't let her be another victim in Anthony's cycle of abuse. The stakes were higher than ever, and I vowed to navigate every legal obstacle, muster every ounce of strength, and protect her from the darkness that Anthony embodied. This battle was no longer just a legal struggle; it was a mission to save Angelina's soul and future.

··· Chapter Seventeen

Every day, I kept my phone glued to my hand, my heart leaped at every buzz and chime, terrified of missing any call or email about Angelina. Each alert from Devra or law enforcement sent a jolt of anxiety through me, a cold sweat breaking out as panic sets in. These feelings never faded; they linger, a constant shadow over my days.

The emails from Devra brought more than just updates—they brought waves of despair. Anthony and his new lawyer had filed yet another appeal to the superior court. Each new appeal felt like a punch to the gut, leaving me feeling hopeless and defeated. It was a relentless rollercoaster of highs and lows, each ascent filled with cautious hope, each descent with crushing despair.Finally, the day of the custody conference arrived. The court system seemed designed to avoid actual hearings, and this conference was intended for modifications to the custody agreement. My goal was clear: I wanted sole legal and physical custody of Angelina. The conference took place on January 11, 2019.

I attended the conference with Devra by my side, having meticulously fulfilled every requirement, from attending seminars for families in conflict to filing my criminal history and abuse verification form. Anthony, on the other hand, was represented by a lawyer but did not bother to attend or complete anything the court had asked of him. The court officer's summary of the conference was a stark recounting of my nightmare:

"In 2015, Father and Mother agreed that Father would take the child to Hungary. Father never left with the child. For a few months, the child stayed with Mother, and then gradually, Father kept the child from Mother. Mother has not seen the child since August 2016. Father has told Mother that he and the child are in the witness protection program, so Mother cannot see the child. In the one year that has passed since the initial custody conference scheduled on Mother's Modification Petition, Mother has not been able to speak with the child. Father reports that she talked with the child in November 2017 and Mother screamed at the child to call her 'Mommy.' Father refused to discuss the case on the merits because of a second pending appeal."

The conference concluded without any resolution, as I had expected. The next step was waiting for the custody trial to be scheduled, a process that could only begin once the Superior Court had denied all of Anthony's appeals.

To afford the mounting attorney bills, I picked up extra hours and on-call shifts at the hospital. My retired parents helped as much as they could, but their resources were limited. Living with them allowed me to funnel my paychecks directly to Devra, but even that wasn't enough. I had to ask Devra for a payment plan. She suggested borrowing money or getting a loan, but I had already filed for bankruptry and my family had given all they could. Eventually, Devra agreed to a payment plan and promised to keep costs low, a gesture for which I was deeply grateful.

Anthony had yet another new lawyer named Ray, who was a friend's brother-in-law. I had met Ray a few times and even watched his children during nursing school. It seemed Anthony cycled through lawyers frequently, likely because they couldn't stomach his immoral actions.

The custody trial was set for March 27, 2019. The wait felt interminable, but by now, I was familiar with the court's slow, methodical process. The order for the custody hearing stated, "The Child at issue shall be brought to the courthouse, along with a responsible adult who will care for the child outside the courtroom during the trial." Finally, Angelina was required to be physically present!

But true to form, Anthony managed to delay the process, claiming an injury to his leg, and the date was pushed to June 3, 2019. I counted down the days with a mix of dread and hope, knowing Anthony would likely try something at the last minute.

By June, my pregnancy was visibly advanced, and it had been a challenging one. I was sick every day, my body swelling with excessive weight and fluid, particularly in my legs. I told Kevin he didn't need to come to the hearing, fearing Anthony's unpredictable nature. My parents and friends accompanied me, providing much-needed support. Anthony's mother and Martin were subpoenaed as well.

June 3, 2019, finally arrived, and we all walked into the courtroom. This time, it wasn't a conference room but an actual courtroom, a setting that felt both intimidating and hopeful. Devra and I took our seats at the table on the right, while Ray sat on the left. Anthony was not there yet. The air was thick with anticipation, the weight of the past years pressing down on me as I prepared for yet another battle in this seemingly endless war.

Behind me, my parents and friends sat, their presence a comforting yet bittersweet reminder of the support I had and the battle we all faced. In front of my parents sat Anthony's mom, a silent figure in this unfolding drama. The familiar faces of the police officer from the other hearings and the court reporter were present, adding to the gravity of the situation. The room's serious tone heightened my nerves, but I kept telling myself that these people were here to help me reclaim my daughter.

In front of me, a pen and tablet lay ready for note-taking, and a glass of water sat within reach. I took a sip, trying to steady my nerves. Devra and I had prepared meticulously for this hearing, and I reminded myself that we were ready.

The judge entered the room, and a hush fell over us.

"Would everyone who is going to be a witness please stand up and be sworn in?" she asked.

The witnesses stood, their solemn faces reflecting the seriousness of the moment. After they were sworn in, the judge addressed Ray.

"Counsel, I notice that the dad is not here. Do you want to tell me what the situation is?"

Ray rose to respond, his voice steady as he began.

"Yes, Your Honor. Your Honor, I had entered my appearance as counsel back in the beginning of January." His words flowed, detailing his initial communications with Anthony and the subsequent request for Anthony to participate telephonically at the custody conference, which had been granted by the judge.

Ray continued, explaining the injury Anthony allegedly sustained, an accident relayed to him through Anthony's wife. His narrative painted a picture of missed communications and unfulfilled responsibilities.

"Since approximately the beginning of March, there was some type of injury, some type of accident, that I was told occurred through his wife, and I have had only one conversation with him since that time," Ray said. qHis frustration was evident as he recounted the lack of communication and the obstacles he faced.

The courtroom was silent except for Ray's voice, each word heightening my anxiety. He described the continuance motion granted due to Anthony's inability to participate, the lack of communication, and the medical issues that supposedly prevented Anthony from traveling.

"I was unable to file any type of pre-trial issue because I had not had the ability to speak with him," Ray admitted. His words underscored the chaotic and evasive nature of Anthony's actions.

Ray detailed the hurdles faced in obtaining Anthony's medical records, citing hospital regulations and Anthony's non-resident status as reasons for the delays.

"We were running into some hurdles at the hospital. They were indicating they couldn't release the record due to Anthony not being a citizen, but being a resident," he explained.

The judge's expression remained impassive, but the weight of the situation was palpable. She interjected, seeking clarification.

"So, he was at the hospital, and they wouldn't release it to him?"

"That is what I am being told, Your Honor, and like I said multiple times, it doesn't make any sense to me." His frustration mirrored my own, each obstacle feeling like another deliberate attempt by Anthony to evade responsibility.

Ray continued, presenting the proxy signed power of attorney and explaining the impossibility of complying with the court's orders due to the bureaucratic and logistical challenges.

"I would just renew my motion for a continuance based upon the fact that according to this paperwork, according to what I was provided today, the medical records were not available. It wasn't possible to have them reviewed by a doctor today to elicit to the Court why he couldn't be here, which is obviously an issue and it's very prejudicial and it's a due process issue as well, Your Honor."

He concluded his plea for a continuance, acknowledging the close timing of the motion to the hearing date and the procedural difficulties.

"If it wasn't for this letter, Your Honor, I would have no real issue to raise before the Court regarding the motion to deny the continuance other than the possibility of doing so according to the rules and the procedure according to Hungary," Ray admitted.

His words hung in the air, a mixture of frustration, procedural complexity, and the stark reality of Anthony's continued absence. Each word felt like another barrier to reuniting with Angelina, the emotional toll pressing down on me. The judge's decision loomed, and I could only hope that justice would finally prevail, bringing me one step closer to my daughter.

"Your Honor, I have had no meaningful communication with my client since February, save for one brief conversation," Ray continued, his voice carrying a note of resignation. "Without the ability to discuss trial tactics or potential settlements, I'm left with nothing but the exhibits and documents presented during last year's hearings. Anthony's position hasn't changed, but I have no new evidence or witnesses to offer today."

The judge maintained an air of impartiality.

"Have you given a copy of that letter to opposing counsel and the court reporter?"

"Yes, Your Honor," Ray replied. "I provided one to opposing counsel and can provide one to the court reporter now."

Before Ray could proceed, Devra intervened, her voice firm and resolute.

"Your Honor, I must state for the record that this letter was only given to me in chambers just before today's hearing. I object to its consideration by the Court. There is no certified translator here to verify its authenticity."

Devra's objections cut through the courtroom air like a knife.

"Anthony's lack of candor with the Court is concerning. We have no confidence these documents are legitimate. There is no proof that he has a mental disorder preventing him from communicating with his attorney. It seems he's hiding behind minimal communication through his wife and dubious medical records related to an old leg injury."

Her words painted a stark picture: Anthony, evading responsibility, hiding in Hungary, using his wife as a shield.

"He has failed to file a pretrial statement, Your Honor, and under the rules, he should be precluded from opposing any claims or defenses or offering any evidence today. He hasn't provided any witness list, exhibit list, or proposed custody order. His attorney admits he's not a resident of Hungary but rather hiding there, keeping my client's child from her."

The judge listened intently.

"Counsel, do you have any witnesses to present today?"

Ray's response was succinct.

"Your Honor, I do not."

The judge's decision was swift.

"I will admit the exhibit for the record so that if this goes up on appeal, we have it. But I do not find it credible or authentic. Even if Anthony's leg was severely injured months ago, it is now June 3rd. It's my experience that someone with such an injury can travel by plane. He could easily arrange a seat with extra legroom. There's no reason his wife couldn't travel with the child. He could testify by phone or video as before. Your motion for continuance is denied. We will proceed."

As I was called for direct examination, Devra began with basic questions about my address, work, and criminal record. She then delved into the painful history of my marriage to Anthony, detailing the physical and mental abuse I endured. Her words brought back the memories of manipulation, coercion, and the traumatic incidents involving other women, including Anthony's current wife, Ethel.

Devra shifted focus to my plans for Angelina, showing the court pictures of our life together: beach trips, holiday celebrations, birthdays, and family outings. Each image was a testament to the love and normalcy I wanted to provide for my daughter. She then presented evidence of my consistent attempts to contact Angelina through texts, emails, and calls to Anthony. She also brought up a letter from the Commonwealth of Pennsylvania that initiated an investigation into my nursing license due to false allegations by Anthony.

"There was no licensing action or discipline taken," Devra clarified.

Devra highlighted Anthony's longstanding non-compliance with a 2017 court order prohibiting him from removing Angelina from Central Pennsylvania and requiring him to surrender her passport.

"Despite multiple notices from his various attorneys, he has failed to comply. We filed a petition of contempt, and my client has incurred significant fees as a result. We request sole legal and physical custody for my client, with immediate transfer of the child under the Hague Convention's enforcement provisions. Anthony's custodial time should be supervised here in Pennsylvania."

Devra turned to me and asked, "Is there anything you'd like to add for the Judge?"

"I just want to see my child," I replied with a trembling voice,

The judge looked at me, a hint of empathy in her eyes.

"I understand."

As I returned to my seat, tears welled up and spilled down my cheeks despite my efforts to remain composed. Devra requested to call the next witness, and the judge turned to my father, identifying the remaining people in the courtroom.

"Who is the woman with the longer brown hair?" the judge asked,

"That's one of Rebecca's friends from Hershey Medical Center and my wife," my dad replied.

"And the woman behind her?"

"That's Anthony's mom," my dad responded.

The judge acknowledged the paternal grandmother's presence and then identified the man in the white shirt.

"What is your name?" Devra asked.

"Martin," he replied, his voice steady.

In that moment, the weight of the situation bore down on all of us, each person playing a role in this unfolding drama, each testimony bringing us closer to a resolution. The battle for Angelina's future continued, with every word and every tear a step towards justice and reunion.

My dad took the witness stand first, a mix of determination and weariness etched on his face. Devra began with the basics, asking him where he resided, with whom, and for how long. As he answered, I realized with a pang of nostalgia that my parents had lived in the same house for thirty years. It was a home filled with memories, both joyous and sorrowful.

"Now, is the subject child in this case, Angelina, your granddaughter?" Devra asked, her tone gentle yet probing.

"Yes, she is," my dad replied, his voice steady but tinged with a sadness that spoke volumes.

"When was the last time you saw her?" Devra continued.

"April of 2015," he answered, his eyes reflecting a deep-seated pain.

Devra dug deeper, asking about his relationship with Angelina. My dad explained how they would see her on holidays, but it was never consistent.

"Anthony would only let Rebecca visit with us sporadically because he was so controlling," he said, his voice breaking slightly. He described the suffocating control Anthony exerted over me, needing to know my every move.

"Now, the relationship that you did have with your granddaughter, when Anthony allowed it—was it loving and close?" Devra asked, her voice softening.

"Well, when we were able to see her, yes," my dad replied. "We were there for her baptism." His eyes lit up momentarily at the memory before the sadness returned.

"Did you observe Rebecca's parenting style?" Devra inquired.

"She was always there for Angelina," my dad said. "If she got a scratch, Rebecca was there to make it better. She took her to different events in Hershey Park. She was with her child."

Next, Anthony's mom was called to the stand. The judge addressed her, reminding her of the importance of truthful testimony. She made her way slowly, needing assistance from the officer to climb the steps. Devra began her questioning, asking when she last saw her granddaughter.

"About a year ago," Anthony's mom replied.

"When was the last time you talked to her?" Devra asked.

"I talk to her all the time," she responded quickly.

"Do you call her?" Devra pressed.

"Yes," she answered.

"When you speak to her, does she speak in English?" Devra continued.

"Yes," she confirmed.

"Does she refer to anyone as 'mommy' when she talks to you?" Devra asked pointedly.

"No," she said, her voice faltering slightly.

"And who does she call 'mommy'?" Devra pressed.

"Ethel," she replied, her voice barely above a whisper.

"Do you know why that is?" Devra asked, her tone direct.

"She has been with her since she was very little," Anthony's mom explained, trying to justify the situation. "I think she remembers her grandmother's daughter."

"Do you know why Anthony isn't here today?" Devra's questions grew more pointed.

Anthony's mom tried to explain an accident involving a ladder, but her words were vague and unconvincing.

"He's really sedated currently," she added.

"I imagine that means he isn't taking care of Angelina?" Devra asked, her voice cold.

"He sees her and stuff, but he is in so much pain," Anthony's mom replied weakly.

Devra's final questions cut to the heart of the matter.

"Have you ever provided Rebecca or her parents with any updates on Angelina?"

"No," Anthony's mom admitted.

"Do you think it's right that Rebecca doesn't get any updates about her child?" Devra asked, her voice rising in intensity.

Anthony's mom turned to me, her eyes hardening.

"No, in a way, but we spoke about this, Rebecca. When you had her, you were always on the phone, and the baby would cry. I told you to pick her up, but you said, 'We don't do that.'"

Devra, her voice dripping with controlled anger.

"All right. Thank you. I have no further questions."

As Anthony's mom stepped down, she yelled to the judge.

"Oh, and by the way, it's not the same leg. It's the other leg."

The judge turned to Devra.

"Do you have any rebuttal testimony?"

"Yes," Devra replied.

At this point, anger simmered within me. I knew Anthony's mom would lie, and her accusations were ridiculous. I took the stand again, my heart pounding in my chest.

"Rebecca, you heard the testimony about you being on the phone all the time. Can you address that?" Devra asked gently.

"I was never constantly on my phone," I replied, my voice shaking with emotion. "I tried to take pictures of my daughter like any mother would, but Anthony didn't want any pictures on Facebook."

"Did you take care of your child?" Devra asked.

"I took care of her most of the time by myself. Anthony's mom helped sometimes, but I was mostly alone while Anthony was out with other women. It was very abusive. I gave Angelina all my love. I am not someone who is on my phone all the time."

The judge looked at me with a mix of empathy and resolve.

"You may step down."

The judge then addressed the court.

"We have an updated Children and Youth report noting the Agency received a GPS regarding the family. Rebecca filed a PFA against Anthony in 2015, which was granted. He tied her up with a curling iron cord and forced her to watch him with the nanny. The child was in the adjacent room. He was charged with terroristic threats and possession of an assault rifle. The file is replete with those issues."

The judge continued to review the factors for custody.

"Father has taken the child to Hungary and not permitted frequent or continuing contact with her mother. The abuse record is clear, and mother has been the primary caregiver. The need for stability and continuity favors the mother. The father has failed to provide emotional support and has been uncooperative."

The judge's voice resonated through the courtroom, each word a beacon of hope, yet laden with the gravity of the situation.

"Based upon the testimony presented today, the Court must review several critical issues. We have a custody issue here, as well as contempt. In our prior opinion, we discussed the judge's order issued just a day or two before this man fled to Hungary. Questions remain as to whether he received the order before leaving the United States. I must review all these details before issuing a contempt order. Additionally, this case has been sent back from the Superior Court to address the abandonment of his appellate counsel on his Superior Court appeal, an issue not addressed today. Now, I must swing back to custody and review the sixteen factors."

The courtroom seemed to hold its breath as the judge continued.

"The first factor is which party is more likely to encourage and permit frequent and continuing contact between the child and the other party. It is clear that the father, having taken the child to Hungary two years ago, has not permitted frequent or continuing contact between the child and her mother. Thus, this factor favors the mother."

She continued.

"The next factor, the abuse issue, is also clear. The record is replete with instances of physical and mental abuse by the father against the mother. Consequently, this factor also favors the mother, who has no history of abuse or any issue of risk of harm to the child."

The judge's words were a balm to my soul, validating the nightmare I had endured.

"In terms of parenting duties, it is evident that when the child was here, the mother was the primary caregiver. If we believe the father's current incapability of even talking on the phone, he is clearly not performing any parental duties. Therefore, this factor favors the mother."

The judge's tone softened a bit as she addressed the need for stability and continuity in the child's education, family life, and community life.

"Every child needs stability. Unfortunately, the child has been in

Hungary, so we need an appropriate transition. I recommend that the mother retain a child psychologist under her insurance to establish an appropriate protocol. There are experts in reunification, including a child psychologist at Harvard who I believe takes Highmark Insurance. Counsel should verify this."

The judge moved on to discuss the availability of extended family.

"The mother has both parents who can assist, while the father has his current wife. This is an equal factor."

When she addressed sibling relationships, my heart sank a bit.

"The parties only have one child. There is no other sibling currently in the child's life."

"The well-reasoned preference of the child, based on her maturity and judgment, is also considered. The child was to appear today as per my court order, confirmed during a telephone conference call. A subpoena was issued, and Dad's counsel accepted service of it. However, she was not brought here. Given her young age and the time she has been kept away from her mother, her stated preference would likely be influenced by the father's and nanny's opinions. Therefore, this factor is irrelevant."

The judge's voice hardened as she addressed the attempts by a parent to turn the child against the other parent.

"We can only surmise that the father has done this. The mother has not. This factor favors the mother."

She then spoke about maintaining a loving, stable, consistent, and nurturing relationship.

"The father has failed to maintain the child's relationship with her biological mother. Therefore, this factor favors the mother."

As she continued, every sentence felt like a step closer to justice.

"Both parties can attend to the daily physical, emotional, developmental, educational, and special needs of the child. However, the father has not attended to her emotional needs by preventing contact with her mother. This factor favors the mother."

"The proximity of the residences is also a significant factor. The mother is in Pennsylvania, while the father is in Hungary. Shared custody is not rational. Furthermore, should the father have custody over the summer, there is no guarantee he would return the child, given his history of absconding. This factor favors the mother."

The judge's assessment of the parents' availability to care for the child or make appropriate childcare arrangements was straightforward.

"Both parents are able to do this. But the level of conflict and willingness to cooperate is another consideration. The father has been obstinate and refuses to cooperate with the mother, as established by the exhibits and testimony. This factor favors the mother."

When addressing the history of drug or alcohol abuse, the judge noted there was no issue in this case.

Finally, the judge discussed the mental and physical condition of each parent.

"The mother has no physical or mental condition affecting her ability to parent. The father's mental condition is questionable, given his false allegations about being in a witness protection program and his abusive behavior. His tying up the mother and forcing her to watch him with another woman is sick. While I don't have a Ph.D. in psychology, it's clear he has issues. His current physical condition allegedly prevents him from caring for a young child. Thus, this factor favors the mother."

The judge concluded.

"The father's behavior in these proceedings is troubling. He has fraudulently transferred real estate titles to avoid judgments. Therefore, we will grant the mother physical custody of the child. The father will have supervised visits at Child First. Both parents shall have legal custody for the next thirty days to allow the father to transport the child back to the mother's physical custody. We will hold another hearing if counsel cannot agree on an appropriate protocol."

"The paternal grandmother and the father's new wife are physically able to return the child. Arrangements should be made, and we will direct an appropriate child custody bond. The mother will need to get the child enrolled in counseling immediately."

As the judge left, Devra turned to me, giving me a reassuring hug. Walking towards my parents, I saw my mom speaking with Anthony's mom. Outside, as we headed to the parking garage, my mom shared what she had said.

"From one grandmother to another, how can you feel this is okay?" Anthony's mom had no response.

Later that week, I received the custody order. The judge's words were a bittersweet victory.

"As set forth in the opinion, I rejected the Father's jurisdictional challenge. The record showed the child had little connection to Pennsylvania since being taken to Hungary. The father's deceitful behavior actively thwarted the mother from maintaining custody rights in Pennsylvania. The father's removal of the child was wrongful, done without the mother's knowledge or consent.

Mother shall have sole legal and physical custody of the child by July 5, 2019. Father will only have supervised visitation.

This was the best news ever, especially with my son due on July 26th. However, my joy was tempered by caution. I knew Anthony would do everything to keep Angelina from me. I daydreamed about her return but feared she wouldn't recognize me.

On May 23, 2019, Kevin and I married at the courthouse. I didn't want Anthony's last name or my maiden name. We knew we were meant to be. We celebrated with a small family dinner at the Hershey Hotel. We found a house outside the city, needing some work before we could move in. On July 21, 2019, our son was born, a healthy, happy baby. We stayed at my parents' house until our new home was ready.

Moving in and starting a new chapter was bittersweet. I returned to work in the fall, our son enrolled in a great daycare. Life began to stabilize, but the custody battle loomed.

With the appeals completed, the contempt hearing was scheduled for July 22, 2020. My judge was no longer serving, which broke my heart. On the hearing day, Anthony's lawyer withdrew. The hearing was stress-free, and the new judge was kind. I sought contempt to eventually move to the federal side.

On August 21, 2020, my petitions for contempt and counsel fees were granted. Anthony was found in civil contempt, ordered to surrender Angelina, pay $4,250 in counsel fees, and face incarceration until he complied. The judge checked "no bail" on the order, a significant victory.

This journey, fraught with pain and struggle, was finally yielding hope. My battle for custody was hard-fought, and the triumph was a testament to my resilience and unwavering love for my daughter.

··· Chapter Eighteen

As I sank into the familiar embrace of my parents' living room, the weight of the recent court battles slowly began to lift. The civil side of the fight was over, and I had won custody. But the victory felt hollow without Angelina by my side. My emotions were a tangled mess—joy and relief at the court's decision mingled with a deep, aching sorrow that my daughter was still so far away. I was elated, but the fear of never seeing her again gnawed at the edges of my happiness.

I wanted to plan a future with Angelina, to imagine the joyous moments we'd share, but a shadow of doubt lingered. *Would Anthony ever cooperate?* The next phase of this battle would be fought on a federal level, and I braced myself for the challenges ahead. Through it all, Devra, my lawyer, had been a beacon of strength and support. She fought fiercely for me, her down-to-earth attitude and genuine care shining through every hug and word of encouragement she offered after each grueling hearing.

Another lawyer at Devra's firm had connections with the district attorney's office, which proved invaluable. She arranged a meeting for me with a local police sergeant to discuss the possibility of pressing criminal charges against Anthony. This meeting was a glimmer of hope in an otherwise daunting landscape.

On September 14, 2020, I walked into the police department, my heart steady. A decade ago, fear would have crippled me, but now, I felt empowered. The police were there to help me, not him. With my friend Katie's prediction about Anthony's behavior echoing in my mind, I knew this was the right step. The sergeant greeted me warmly and escorted me to a small, stark room. I shared my story, struggling to condense the years of pain and deception into a "short" version. My goal was clear: pursue criminal charges and bring my daughter home.

To my relief, the sergeant spoke with the district attorney, who agreed to charge Anthony. On September 17, 2020, felony charges were issued for Interference with Custody of Children and Concealment of Whereabouts of Child. The sergeant called to inform me that Anthony would be arrested and that the US Marshals and FBI were involved. It felt like the pieces were finally falling into place.

But then, on November 11, 2020, another call brought news that Homeland Security and the FBI were now leading the case, as the US Marshals claimed no jurisdiction. Patience became my constant companion as I awaited updates, my heart heavy with anticipation and dread. The FBI tracked Anthony's passport, revealing his movements between the US and Europe. The last documented date for Angelina's passport showed she was in the United States on December 1, 2017. This information, though fragmented, was a lifeline.

Out of the blue, Yvette, the wife of Anthony's childhood friend Joey, reached out. A reporter had asked her about Angelina, and she was shocked by the story I shared. Yvette was horrified and offered her help, revealing that Anthony had dropped Angelina off at their house abruptly in June 2020. She had babysat Angelina two years ago, and her husband had recent pictures of her, though he refused to share them with Yvette. She contacted her local police, providing them with the warrants against

Anthony. We hoped to catch Anthony if he returned to the US and stayed with Joey. It was a fragile strategy, but it was something.

In August 2021, Anthony applied for services at the US Embassy in Hungary, triggering alerts. Agents prepared to take him into custody, but he did not show up. Later, he attempted again, and although his passport was confiscated, he was not detained. It was unclear if he had gone to the embassy himself or sent his wife. Without a passport, Anthony was stuck in Hungary.

On October 26, 2021, Anthony's criminal attorney met with the district attorney. The attorney suggested dropping all charges so Anthony could return to the US to discuss custody. I refused. The only deal I would consider was if Anthony returned under US Marshal supervision with Angelina and handed her over to me, with court-supervised visits only. Otherwise, the felony charges would stand.

Anthony might still believe he could manipulate the system or buy his way out. But this time, he was cornered. No amount of money or deceit could change the fact that justice was on our side. The fight was far from over, but I was ready to see it through to the end.

On November 11, 2021, I received an e-mail very early in the morning while I was getting ready for work. This email was written by a Hungarian lawyer.

> "Dear Madam, I am writing you on behalf of Anthony. As you know yourself and my client's common minor child, Angelina (born in Hershey on 23, April 2012 US citizen) relocated to Hungary and Angelina has been living with the father's new family since the year 2015. My client wishes you to have known Angelina. She is a great child who deserves to have some contact with her mother. She is an honor student in school as well on the horse-riding team and judo club and art classes. I would like to build a relationship between you and your daughter with the consent of the father first via skype and then personally. I would like you to participate in the Hungarian legal

procedure. There is a mediation program where you and the father can reach an agreement on the method and timing of your contact with Angelina. Please let me know your attention where you would be willing to participate in that procedure and made and agreement with the father in a legal procedure before the District Court of Kecskemet."

When I first read the letter, my heart skipped a beat. It seemed too good to be true. Anthony would never willingly let me speak to Angelina. His motives were clear; he wanted to manipulate me into complying with the Hungarian court system, ultimately stripping me of any legal rights or custody here in the United States. Anthony was grasping at straws, desperate to get his passport back to continue his mysterious ventures. The letter claimed she had moved to Hungary in 2015, a blatant lie since I last saw her in August 2016. I forwarded the letter to the Sergeant, who confirmed its authenticity through Anthony's attorney. The district attorney wanted to meet with me to discuss the next steps in bringing my daughter home.

Anthony had flouted court orders, restricting my time with Angelina and engaging in blatant parental alienation. The thought of what lies and negative comments he might have fed her was unbearable. I feared for her emotional well-being, praying she wouldn't struggle with self-esteem and guilt. The pain of parental alienation was indescribable, a daily torment that left a gaping void in my heart.

Parental kidnapping leaves scars that run deep. Children who are abducted face a higher risk of psychological issues—anxiety, mood disorders, aggressive behavior, and eating disorders. As adults, they often grapple with identity, relationships, and family issues. The longer a child is gone, the more challenging reunification becomes. Yet, I was ready, mentally and physically, to face these challenges when Angelina returned.

While some might be paralyzed by such a traumatic event, I found myself driven to resolve the situation. Weekly, I called and emailed the sergeant and the assistant district attorney, seeking updates. The prolonged process was maddening, leading to frustration, hopelessness, depression, and anger. I couldn't fathom why there wasn't more urgency, why this wasn't recognized as an emergency. I had no updates on Angelina's safety or health, no new pictures or videos. All I had was the last photo from August 1, 2016, of her smiling in front of the sunflowers we planted.

Living this nightmare, I carry immense guilt from the day I returned to Anthony, leaving my cousin's house. That was my chance to escape with Angelina, and I missed it. The word resilience became my mantra. I had been knocked down countless times, but I found ways to emotionally heal and continue my mission to bring Angelina home. I maintained a positive attitude, believing that each setback was just a sign to try a different path.

Angelina turned ten on April 23, 2022, and she remained in Hungary. The Russian invasion of Ukraine on February 24, 2022, added to my fears. If Angelina was in Kecskemét, she was only fourteen hours away from Kyiv. The thought of her being in the path of war was agonizing. If Anthony had any sense, he would return to the United States and make a deal.

Despite the years without my daughter, I refuse to give up. Financial constraints were a constant worry, but somehow, things always worked out. I couldn't afford to fight overseas in Hungary, but I had won here in the United States. My family and friends were my pillars of support, and my husband helped me rediscover myself after years of abuse. Learning to relax, meditate, pray, and manifest positive thoughts became essential for my well-being. My friend Lisa was instrumental in helping me focus on the future rather than the past. Self-care became a vital tool in my recovery from an abusive relationship.

After fourteen years with a narcissist, finding happiness was crucial for healing. My peaceful morning routine of exercise and coffee, scheduling massages, hair, or nail appointments, all became acts of self-love. Physically, I had to recover from the long-term effects of abuse. Severe nerve damage in my wrist required surgery, and I had to undergo procedures to fix my deviated septum. Chronic back and neck pain, along with migraines, were constant reminders of my past, but I sought treatment and continued to push forward.

Despite these setbacks, stress lingered, its grip tight until I knew Angelina was safe and home. Every day, I wonder about her well-being. *Is she happy and healthy? Does she remember me? How is she doing in school? Does she have friends? Could she find a way to contact me?*

Every night, I pray for her safe return, whispering, "Please God, help bring my daughter home."

Please.

Bring the girl home.

About the Author

Rebecca Wilson is an acclaimed author, registered nurse, advocate and survivor whose remarkable journey has shaped her into a leading voice in the fight against domestic violence and familial kidnapping. With unflinching honesty and raw emotion, in Bring the Girl Home: Surviving Domestic Violence and an International Kidnapping Rebecca shares her own harrowing story of resilience, hope and the relentless pursuit to reunite with her daughter. Through her powerful narrative, she shines a light on the dark reality of abuse, exposing its devastating impact of individuals and families. By sharing her deeply personal experience, Rebecca aims to break the silence and stigma surrounding domestic violence, inspiring others to find their strength and break free from the cycle of violence.

Rebecca firmly believes in the power of education, community engagement, and open dialogue as essential tools in combatting domestic violence. She actively engages in advocating for increased awareness, prevention and support for survivors. Her unwavering dedication to this cause is earning her recognition as a leading advocate and a beacon of hope for countless individuals facing similar challenges.

In addition to her advocacy work, Rebecca finds solace and rejuvenation in spending time outdoors with her husband, son and two dogs. Whether hiking through serene forests, kayaking along tranquil rivers, or simply enjoying the beauty of a sunset, these moments remind her of the resilience and beauty of life. Through her writing, advocacy and personal journey, she continues to inspire and empower others to find their voice, stand against injustice, and create a world where violence no longer has a place.